The Six Sigma Journey from Art to Science

A Business Novel

To my neighbors Ray & Joyce
Thanks for listening.

Larry Walters

Also available from ASQ Quality Press:

Six Sigma Project Management: A Pocket Guide
Jeffrey N. Lowenthal

Six Sigma for the Shop Floor: A Pocket Guide
Roderick A. Munro

Customer Centered Six Sigma: Linking Customers, Process Improvement, and Financial Results
Earl Naumann and Steven H. Hoisington

Lean Enterprise: A Synergistic Approach to Minimizing Waste
William A. Levinson and Raymond A. Rerick

The Memory Jogger Plus
Michael Brassard

Managing Change: Practical Strategies for Competitive Advantage
Kari Tuominen

Improving Performance through Statistical Thinking
ASQ Statistics Division

The Desk Reference of Statistical Quality Methods
Mark L. Crossley

To request a complimentary catalog of ASQ Quality Press publications, call 800-248-1946, or visit our Web site at http://qualitypress.asq.org .

The Six Sigma Journey from Art to Science

A Business Novel

Larry Walters

ASQ Quality Press
Milwaukee, Wisconsin

The Six Sigma Journey from Art to Science
Larry Walters

Library of Congress Cataloging-in-Publication Data

Walters, Larry, 1958–
  The six sigma journey from art to science : a business novel / Larry
Walters.
     p. cm.
  ISBN 0-87389-552-5 (pbk. : alk. paper)
  1. Quality control—Fiction. 2. Pigments industry—Fiction. 3. Six
Sigma (Quality control standard)—Fiction I. Title.

PS3623.A448 S59 2002
813'.6—dc21   2002007240

10 9 8 7 6 5 4 3 2 1

ISBN 0-87389-552-5

Acquisitions Editor: Annemieke Koudstaal
Project Editor: Craig S. Powell
Production Administrator: Jennifer Czajka
Special Marketing Representative: David Luth

ASQ Mission: The American Society for Quality advances individual,
organizational, and community excellence worldwide through learning,
quality improvement, and knowledge exchange.

Attention Bookstores, Wholesalers, Schools, and Corporations: ASQ Quality
Press books, videotapes, audiotapes, and software are available at quantity
discounts with bulk purchases for business, educational, or instructional use.
For information, please contact ASQ Quality Press at 800-248-1946, or write to
ASQ Quality Press, P.O. Box 3005, Milwaukee, WI 53201-3005.

To place orders or to request a free copy of the ASQ Quality Press Publications
Catalog, including ASQ membership information, call 800-248-1946. Visit our
Web site at www.asq.org or http://qualitypress.asq.org .

Printed in the United States of America

♾ Printed on acid-free paper

American Society for Quality

Quality Press
600 N. Plankinton Avenue
Milwaukee, Wisconsin 53203
Call toll free 800-248-1946
Fax 414-272-1734
www.asq.org
http://qualitypress.asq.org
http://standardsgroup.asq.org
E-mail: authors@asq.org

This book is dedicated to quality professionals working to make their business a better place for their customers and fellow workers. And to all the people that have taken the time to help me learn and understand the "real world."

Table of Contents

List of Characters   ix

Preface   xi

Chapter 1   It's an Art, Not a Science   1

Chapter 2   Decision Making   11

Chapter 3   Career Progression   15

Chapter 4   Economics   19

Chapter 5   The Visionary   21

Chapter 6   Problems, Problems, Problems   27

Chapter 7   Cleveland Bound   33

Chapter 8   Six Sigma in Action   41

Chapter 9   The Big Sell   59

Chapter 10   The Leader   71

Chapter 11   Step Up to the Plate   79

Chapter 12   The Plan   83

Chapter 13   Executive Training Begins   87

Chapter 14   Executive Training: Define and Measure   97

Chapter 15   Executive Training: Analyze   105

Chapter 16   Executive Training: Improve   111

Chapter 17   Executive Training: Control   125

Chapter 18   The Decision   129

Chapter 19   Setting the Stage   133

Chapter 20   Our Event   141

Chapter 21   The Big Rumor   147

Chapter 22   People Really Do Care   151

Chapter 23   The Blackbelts   153

Chapter 24   The Auction   159

Chapter 25   Blackbelt Training: Define and Measure   163

Chapter 26   Blackbelt Training: Analyze   169

Chapter 27   Blackbelt Training: Improve   175

Chapter 28   Blackbelt Training: Control   183

Chapter 29   The Results Roll In   187

Chapter 30   Certification   193

Chapter 31   Three Months Later   199

List of Characters

Although this book is reasonably brief, the list of characters is long. This is because a good Six Sigma implementation involves a lot of people. To help the reader keep track of the characters, a summary of the major characters is included here for easy reference.

Barry Watson—Head of the quality department at HPZ Chemicals and a member of the management team. Responsible for the Six Sigma implementation at HPZ Chemicals.

Bob Jones—New division president of HPZ Chemicals' parent company, HPZ Holdings, and true leader.

Charlie—Plant manager for HPZ Chemicals.

Dave—Master Blackbelt from Six Sigma Enterprises.

Ed—Six Sigma Blackbelt working for Maintenance.

Henry—VP of finance at HPZ Chemicals.

Howard—Engineering manager at HPZ Chemicals.

Jack—President of HPZ Chemicals.

James—Six Sigma Blackbelt working for Howard in Engineering.

Jimmy—VP of sales at HPZ Chemicals.

Julie—Six Sigma Blackbelt working for Mark in R&D.

Lou—Area production manager for HPZ Chemicals.

Mark—VP of research and development at HPZ Chemicals.

Pat—ISO coordinator working for Barry.

Paula—Six Sigma Blackbelt working for Henry in Finance.

Rodney—Six Sigma Blackbelt working in Operations as production foreman.

Roman—Master Blackbelt from Six Sigma Enterprises.

Russ Peterson—VP of quality for Nutech Industries and Six Sigma visionary.

Sarah—Six Sigma Blackbelt and lab manager working for Barry.

Steve—VP of manufacturing at HPZ Chemicals.

Tim—Six Sigma Blackbelt working for Mark in R&D.

Preface

As a member of the quality profession, I became very excited when I was first exposed to Six Sigma. I'm still excited. It answered so many questions about so many things I had experienced during my 20-year business career. Ultimately though, I became frustrated because it was so difficult to share the concepts with the people that needed them most. A textbook approach to Six Sigma just did not allow people to understand Six Sigma's true value. I felt a motivational approach utilizing a business novel format might work better. Plus it would be more enjoyable to read.

Equally frustrating for me was the belief of many companies that putting a couple of people through Six Sigma training would, by itself, somehow transform their company from a loser into a winner. And if it did not, then Six Sigma was not what it was made out to be. To those companies wanting a quick and easy solution to their problems, keep looking, Six Sigma is not the solution.

I have seen Six Sigma transform itself into a big global business. If you can spell Six Sigma these days, it seems you are qualified to teach it. Like anything else, the buyer must beware. If it sounds too easy, costs too little, and promises too much—think again. Six Sigma will not solve all of your problems. It is not a cure for poor management, and it won't work without a qualified and motivated workforce. With Six Sigma, the reward you receive is directly proportional to the effort you exert. I know consulting companies have a hard time saying "no" if offered a business opportunity. It won't be hard to find someone to promise you what you want to hear. Hopefully this book will help you ask the right questions, not only to your consultants but also to yourself.

It is also my hope that this book will help people understand what it means and takes to implement this thing we call Six Sigma. And the rewards it can bring. I also hope it will be an inspiration for those people trying to make things better; don't give up. For some companies though, implementing Six Sigma, with their current set of problems, might be exactly the wrong thing to do. Or, the wrong time to do it. Six Sigma is really one of those things you have to do right the first time—there won't be a second time.

I have attempted to keep the book brief so that the reader's valuable time is not wasted. Although many of the examples and the setting are manufacturing-based, most readers will realize that all types of businesses and work processes can benefit from Six Sigma. To try and include some example from every type of work practice would create the opposite of the intention of the book, which is a simple and easy-to-read introduction to Six Sigma.

The people and events of this book are fictional. I think many people will recognize traits of someone they know, but this is coincidental.

I sincerely hope that your Six Sigma Journey from Art to Science will be a successful and satisfying one.

1

It's an Art, Not a Science

It was 1985. The U.S. economy was doing well and companies were making money. HPZ Chemicals had made me a nice offer and I went straight from school to work without missing a beat. My first month as an engineer consisted of training, trying to look busy, and meeting people who weren't too excited to be working at HPZ.

HPZ Chemicals Inc. was a medium sized chemical plant that produced catalysts, dyes, and pigments. It was a part of HPZ Holdings, which made a lot of products. Our plant was one was the largest in the corporation and had been in business a lot longer than I had been alive.

So far I had found little that my education had prepared me to do in the real world. Some of the people who were training me didn't seem to know much more than I did. I guess I expected a big company to be better organized.

So I was nervous, but excited, when my boss called me to his office. Maybe I would get to do something other than learn how to fill out the proper paperwork.

As I approached the door, I looked in the window of Mr. Raymond Jebson's office. He was poring intently over a pile of papers on his desk. I knocked on the door.

"Come in," said Raymond. He looked up from the papers and motioned for me to enter. Raymond looked like a science teacher I had in high school. But everyone looked like that with the safety glasses we had to wear.

"Pull up a chair," he smiled and motioned to a chair in front of his desk.

As I sat down, he said, "I've got a special job for you, if you think you are ready." He emphasized the word "you".

"I think I'm ready," I replied trying to sound confident.

"We have a test scheduled in Plant One over the next few days starting tomorrow and we need to cover it around the clock."

"OK," I said apprehensively.

"We need someone to cover the midnight shift. That is, if you want to?" The way he said it, I knew I was expected to cover the midnight shift.

"I can do midnights," I said trying to sound as confident as I could.

"Working midnights won't bother you will it?"

"Oh no," I replied. "I think it will be exciting."

"Well, I don't know about exciting. If you run into problems you will have a number to call."

"So, it will be just me on midnights?" It came out a little higher pitched than normal.

"Unless that's a problem?" Raymond asked sounding serious.

"No, not at all." I swallowed hard and gave him my most confident look.

"Great, I will have Bill come and explain what you will be doing and show you around the area. You know Bill don't you?"

"Yes sir, we met the other day."

"OK, well Bill will get with you this afternoon. Good luck on the midnights. Try and get some sleep tomorrow before you come in." Mr. Jebson looked back down at his papers.

I got up and said, "Thanks," as I left the office.

I went back to my office and started to study some drawings I had been given. The drawings had been rolled up for years, and I had a hard time keeping them flat. Welcome to the real world I told myself.

"Hey, how ya doing?"

I jumped at the sound of Bill's voice. I had been so intent at studying the drawings on my desk, I hadn't heard him come in.

"Sorry, didn't mean to spook ya." Bill was an elderly gentleman with a slow southern drawl.

"That's OK," I said. "I was trying to figure out these flow sheets."

He leaned over and looked at what I was studying.

"Who gave you those?" He had a frown on his face.

"Training department," I said apprehensively.

"Figures," he chuckled. "They're not up to date. Those things are as old as me," he said smiling. "I'll get some up-to-date ones if we have them. We don't have current drawings on everything though."

"That would be great." So I have been wasting my time studying the wrong stuff, I thought.

"Hear you're gonna be helping us out."

"Huh?"

"The test, you know the one Raymond spoke to ya about."

"Oh, the test! Yeah, sure, I guess. If I know how to do what you want me to do that is."

"Don't worry about that. We don't expect you to be able to do much until you've been here a while. It'll take you five years to understand how this place works."

Five years, I thought to myself. Wow.

"Hey, you had lunch yet?"

"Not yet," I said.

"We'll talk about what I need ya to do, and when we get back I'll take ya out in the plant and show you where to take the readings."

"Sounds good to me," I said as we headed down the steps.

After lunch, we headed back to Bill's office. I thought Raymond's office was messy, but Bill's office looked like a junkyard. It was overflowing with papers, and there were parts and valves and gauges and lab equipment everywhere. We could barely get both of us into the office. Bill moved a pile of papers from a chair to the floor and motioned for me to sit down.

"What's that?" I pointed to something that looked like an old tent.

"That's an old filter cloth. Failed early on us and I'm sending it back to the supplier to see if they can tell us why it failed."

"Does that happen often?"

"All the time."

"Oh?" I replied. "Does it cause lots of problems when it fails?"

"Well, slows us down a lot when we stop to replace it, but it's just the nature of the stuff we make. Sometimes they last a month, sometimes three, sometimes more. Some seem to work better than others."

"Sounds like a big problem."

"Ah, it's just one of those things. We got a million little things that bug us like that all the time. You can't figure out everything, not enough time or people."

"Oh?" I replied, a little surprised.

Bill leaned back in his chair. It went back so far I thought he was going to tip over. He looked over his glasses at me. "OK, here's what we gotta do the next few days. I got this project to install a baghouse and save us some money on #1 mill but we need to see if she'll feed OK using a baghouse, and make sure the quality doesn't deteriorate. So I piped the baghouse from #4 and got it set up on #1 mill. The thing might pressurize, I don't know, so we're gonna give it a try and see what happens."

I looked at Bill and nodded my head up and down but I didn't have a clue what he was talking about. It sure didn't sound very scientific to me though.

"So you're gonna be on midnights. I'll be on days with Tony. Craig will do the afternoon shift."

"OK. What will I actually be doing?"

"Taking readings and samples and just making sure everything goes OK. Just be there in case production has a question. If no one's there to answer their questions, production will just do what they want to."

I thought that surely the production people knew how to do their jobs. I was not sure what he meant by "they will just do what they want to."

"If you have any problems, give me a call at home. Here's my home phone number." He handed me a slip of paper.

"Sounds good to me." At least I had the phone number of someone who knew what was going on. I stuck it in my pocket.

"Now let's go out in the plant and I'll show you what to do."

I followed Bill out into the plant. We had our hard hats and safety glasses on. He showed me the gages to read and showed me a log sheet to fill out. After we had gone through the area, I felt a little better. I still wasn't clear on what we were actually trying to accomplish with the test but I knew what I had to do. I wasn't sure why they needed an engineer to do it. It was really kind of simple.

Back in the office, we took off our hats and wiped the sweat off our faces. It was pretty hot in the plant, and very noisy. I noticed Bill was relatively clean while I was dirty.

"So you got it?" Bill asked.

"I think so, but it doesn't seem like it's very scientific what we are trying to do," I replied cautiously.

"Oh, that's just because you aren't used to things in the real world. Stuff you learn in school doesn't apply out here in the plant. Best way to find things out is trial and error; try it, see what works. Making pigment is an art, not a science. You'll find out what I mean after you've been here a while." He spoke to me like a father would speak to a son.

He continued, "OK, so we'll see you tomorrow at 11 p.m. in Craig's office. You will be relieving him. And Tony and I will relieve you at 7 a.m. Friday morning. Any problems, give me a call; you've got my number. Any questions?"

"I've just got one."

"Shoot."

"How did I get so dirty when you're so clean?" I laughed.

Bill laughed back. "That's something else you will learn after you have been here for a while."

Bill continued to tell me how things were in the real world and not to expect it to match what I had learned in school. I didn't really understand why, but he had been an engineer for 25 years and I had one month under my belt. I waved good-bye and headed for my car.

The next night I was back to work. The plant had a different feel to it late at night. The smoke from the stacks drifted across the dark sky, but it was clearly visible because of the thousands of lights used to illuminate the plant. And it was way too quiet on the graveyard shift.

I made my way up the steps to Craig's office and saw him at his desk.

"Hi, Craig," I said as I walked into his office.

"Hi, Barry," he said as he glanced nervously at his watch. It was nearly 11:00 p.m.

"How is the test going?" I asked.

"Hasn't even got running good yet. They had problems on day shift and I've been waiting on maintenance all shift. So check in with the production foreman and he will give you the scoop. I'm out of here." With that Craig grabbed his hat and left me standing there with my mouth hanging open.

I watched him leave the building and then read the notes in the logbook. The log sheet had a couple of readings but none since day shift. I hoped I could find the foreman's office again.

I walked down the hall, peering in offices, looking for the production foreman. Bill had shown me the office earlier, and I was sure it was this way. I heard voices down the hall and saw a light on. There was a tag on the door that said "Production." Must be the place.

I peeked around the corner and saw a man sitting at a desk with his feet up and two guys standing in front of him. The man behind the desk was staring at the ceiling. He had on jeans and a flannel shirt and work boots. He had a disgusted look on his face.

That's when they noticed me standing at the door.

"Who are you?" asked a guy holding the biggest pipe wrench I had ever seen.

"Hi, my name is Barry. I'm on the midnight shift covering the . . ."

The guy behind the desk cut me off before I could answer and said, "So you're the sucker Bill got to cover midnights, huh?"

"Well, yeah I guess so." I wasn't sure what to say.

"Hi, my name is Glenn," said the foreman behind the desk. He stuck out his hand while taking his feet off the desk.

"Hi, I'm Barry," I said, and shook his hand.

"This is Butch and Darrell," he said pointing to the two other guys in the office. "They're in maintenance."

"How's it going?" said the one with the pipe wrench.

"Not bad," I said as I shook both of their hands.

"Welcome to the graveyard shift," Butch said, raising his eyebrows at me. He had on a pair of dirty work pants and a shirt with "Butch" stitched on it. He looked a little on the rough side.

"Thanks. Can you tell me what's going on with Bill's test?" I asked apprehensively.

Glenn answered, "Well, Butch and Darrell here are gonna try and get the bucket elevator fixed so we can run the stupid test. Chain jumped the sprocket and last shift spent the entire time digging out the elevator. But I can tell you it ain't gonna work."

"Why is that?" I asked, thinking Glenn might have some knowledge I needed to know.

"Tried that same thing three years ago. Didn't work then, won't work now. Stuff that works at other places won't work here. This is a pigment plant. Making pigment is an art, not a science. They can't teach you how to make this stuff in school, can they guys?" Butch and Darrell nodded their heads in agreement.

"Uh, well, I don't know about all that, I'm just supposed to take some readings and get samples when it is running." It seemed a lot of people thought this plant was more art than science.

"Tell you what. Give me your extension and we'll call ya when we get it up and running," Glenn said with a slight air of superiority. "Listen to us old production guys and we will teach you what really goes on out here."

"I'll be at extension 1243."

"I'll call as soon as we get her up and running."

Most of the night was me checking on Glenn checking on maintenance. At 3 a.m., I was wondering if I should call Bill at home but decided he could not do anything about it. Maintenance was working on it. I wondered why Glenn was so sure the test would be a failure. I decided to ask Bill the next morning. At 4:00 a.m., I got a call from Glenn saying they were up and running again.

I hurried out with my clipboard and took the readings Bill had told me to get. I also got the samples of product, being sure to label them with the date and time and my initials. I was happy to have something to do, and the time went by much faster. Before I knew it, it was 7 a.m. and Bill was walking in the door.

"How'd it go last night?" he asked.

"They had maintenance problems so I only got two samples."

"Figures. This plant seems to know when you want to try something new."

"Bill," I asked, "Glenn seemed to think this test would not work because we had done this three years ago and it failed then."

"He's right, but we thought we'd try it again. A lot of pressure from corporate to reduce costs these days."

"But if we already tried it and it didn't work?" I asked.

"Don't mean it won't work this time. Remember what I told you, making pigment is an art, not a science. Besides we gotta do something to meet the corporate goals. We've been making this stuff for 25 years, everything new has been pretty much tried before anyway."

I remember falling into bed when I got home around 8 a.m. I had been up for over 24 hours. The last thing I remember before I passed out was thinking to myself, "Why is it an art, not a science. Don't the laws of science apply here?"

I also found out another reason why they call it the graveyard shift. You sleep like you are dead after the first night.

2

Decision Making

I worked the midnight shift three more nights during which time the equipment was down as often as it was running. The samples collected during the test were submitted to the lab and Bill compiled the data. We had a meeting scheduled to review the experiment at 10 a.m. and the rest of the department was going to be there.

The meeting was in the production conference room. There was an overhead projector and a whiteboard. When I walked in the room, my boss, Raymond, was writing something on the board. He turned around as I entered the room.

"Hey Barry, glad to see you survived the midnight shift."

"Yeah, me too." I was exhausted. Midnights were to be avoided I had decided. It was pretty rough on your body changing your sleep cycle around like that. I hoped I would not have too many of those in my future.

"Rest of the folks will be here soon. Have a seat. How did you like working in the plant?"

"It was different." I didn't want to tell him the truth.

"Yeah, if you never worked in a plant like this one before, it can be a bit intimidating," he smiled at me.

"I'll get used to it."

"Well, we need people who know the process and how the plant really operates, so learn all you can and you might go places out here. Give it a few more years and you will be running these tests by yourself."

I sat down and watched as the rest of the department came in. Along with our department were the area production manager and the plant manager. I introduced myself to them as the room started to fill up.

Charlie was the plant manager. He had been at the plant for 25 years. Helped to build the place. The area manager was Lou, who was known to be a character. Our department consisted of Raymond, Bill, Tony, Craig, George, and Donald. Everyone had warned me about George. He was a grouchy old engineer who thought he knew everything. And then there was Donald, the engineer who didn't *think* he knew everything, he was *sure* he knew everything.

"Thanks for coming to the meeting," Raymond said. "We want to review the results of the test and get everyone's input. Bill will review the data."

Bill stood up and meandered to the front of the room. He had several overhead transparencies. He looked up at everyone and said, "Well things didn't go exactly as we had planned."

"Your tests never do," said Lou.

Bill just went on like he had not heard him.

"We ran with the baghouse in place and it appears to improve the recovery like we hoped. I have the test data here to see if it impacted quality."

Bill turned on the overhead and a graph with dots and lines appeared on the screen behind him. I couldn't see much, but Bill started pointing out what he said were trends.

"Ya see here is where we started and things were OK. Then the quality went worse here but got a little better at the end."

"What happened to make it better and then worse?" asked Charlie.

"We don't know," said Bill.

"What happened before the run where it dipped down?" asked Tony, who was scrunching up his face trying to see something. I didn't see anything, but I wasn't sure what I was looking at anyway. These guys had 100 years of experience between them and I sure wasn't going to question them.

"That's when we brought in that new raw material," said George.

"Yeah, had to be that. We didn't change anything else," said Charlie.

Bill next placed a table of numbers on the overhead.

"Here is the average of the quality before, during, and after the test. As you can see, during the test the average residue level is higher than before and after the test, so the quality was definitely poorer during the test."

I was having some problems understanding everything but the average during the test was larger, though not by much.

"Based on the quality deterioration we saw, I recommend we don't make this change" said Bill. "It's a shame because we might have saved some money, but it just didn't work the way we had hoped."

The group got up from the table and headed in their own separate ways.

I caught Bill on the way out and asked him how he was sure that the test was a failure.

"Well," Bill said, scratching his head, "you never really know anything for sure Barry. All you can do is look at what you get and make your best decision. That's why we get the other folks like Charlie and Lou in there because they've seen it all. They have a lot of experience making this stuff and you can't learn that in a book. You have to use your gut instinct on these things. Plus, we kind of thought the residue would be higher anyway."

"Oh?" I said, surprised.

"Don't forget Barry, making pigment is an art, not a science. Things that work everywhere else won't work here. This is a complicated plant. It takes years to learn this place and how to make pigment. Just keep your ears open and learn all you can. We need folks who know how to make pigment."

I wondered just how long it would take me to be able to acquire the instincts to make decisions like these guys.

As Bill walked down the hall, I called after him.

"Hey Bill!"

"What?" he turned to answer.

"How much money would be saved if this had worked?"

"Half a million dollars a year." He turned back towards his office.

"Half a million a year?" I said out loud. Too bad the test failed.

3

Career Progression

For the next fifteen years I worked in a variety of positions within the organization. I had just recently been promoted to quality manager and had been put on the operations management team. I shared in the management activities of the plant. This meant I came to work each morning not knowing what problem had surfaced since my absence, and I spent each day trying to figure out how to make it disappear before the next problem came along. A few times each year the process seemed to run smoothly and this was a time enjoyed by all—but it never lasted. I often thought how nice it would be if we could really understand what made the process run smoothly.

"Hey Tony, why is everything running so well this week? I've actually had time to sit down and catch up on my e-mail and get my reports finished on time." Tony worked for me now and he was a valuable member of my group.

"Who knows? Better enjoy it while it lasts because the next fire is just over the horizon and we might be out here all night again."

"Have you ever thought what it would be like to know what causes this place to go crazy?"

"I already know."

"Really?" I asked in amazement.

"Yeah, people don't do their job."

"Really, what people?"

"Maintenance, production, management, everybody." He said it like this was obvious.

"I don't buy that," I replied.

"Why not?"

"I've been here 15 years now and I see the same stuff happen over and over. But it doesn't always happen. What causes it to start and what causes it to stop? Somebody ought to know by now."

"People don't do their jobs, I told you." Tony replied emphatically.

"People might be part of it, but what about when the quality goes off? First thing we do is start taking extra samples to be tested. Then we wait on the results. Then we take some more samples. Then we might make a small change and wait to see what happens. If that doesn't fix it we change something else. Next thing you know the problem goes away and we claim the last thing we changed fixed it."

Tony replied, "That's true, but the thing that really makes me mad is when you try and do something better, and then if anything in the whole plant gets worse, you get blamed for it." Tony was getting upset now too. Tony continued, "Remember when we tried that new supplier's product in the back end of the plant, the one that was going to save us a bunch of money."

"Oh yeah, that was when the activity of the catalyst went low and they blamed it on that supplier. I felt so bad for him. He spent all that time and you know, when we kicked him out the problem didn't go away."

"Yeah, there are still people that say that stuff caused us problems. I had a call from him the other day. He said purchasing wouldn't even talk to him. He was going to save us a bunch of money too!" Tony said angrily.

"That's exactly what I'm talking about," I said. "I've been doing some research."

"How's that?" said Tony.

"Well, I've been looking at how we fix things out here. We have a problem, so we make a change to fix the problem, and the next time the same thing happens we make the same change but it doesn't fix it. Even worse, look at this. Here is a list of the changes we made in the process in the last six months."

Tony leaned over and looked at the sheet on my desk.

"See how we seem to be always making the same changes. Sometimes we change something to fix a problem and then change it right back to fix the same problem."

"What do you mean?" Tony was starting to get interested now.

"Well, look here at this change on April 22. We had filtration problems so we raised the pH from 7.0 to 7.5. Supposedly the problem went away so we changed the operating specification. Now look here on June 3. It says the pH was too high and was causing filtration problems. So what did we do? We lowered the specification back to 7.0 and supposedly the problem went away. That can't be right!"

"I see what you mean now. How can making the pH higher correct the same problem as lowering it back to where it was? I guess that's why you need to work out here so many years to be able to run this place. Everyone always says it's an art and not a science."

"Well, I'm starting to get tired of hearing that. Why should this place be any different than any other plant?"

"The people I talk to from other plants seem to have the same types of problems we have. Maybe all the other plants in the world are like this too."

"I just don't believe that Tony. Maybe it's only an art because we aren't smart enough to figure out what is really going on."

"No way. As many years as we have been doing this we have it figured out as good as anybody. It's just a hard process, that's all."

"I used to think so, but I'm not so sure now. Do you know what it's like to get called up front to explain some problem when you don't have a clue what is going on? Then when it goes away, they pat you on the back and say 'good job Barry.' You don't have the nerve to tell them you have no idea as to why it got better. So you just say the changes you made fixed it. You know, maybe I shouldn't show this stuff to anyone else."

"I think you're right Barry. Let's just keep it our secret."

That night I went home, grabbed a beer from the refrigerator and headed out on the deck. The conversation with Tony was really bothering me. I really was starting to feel stupid. I remembered back to when I had first started working for HPZ and how scared I was that I wouldn't know what to do. It was 15 years later and I still felt the same way. How can you work at a place for 15 years and not know everything there was to know about it? It was a complicated process but I was sure there were plenty of things a lot more complicated than what we did.

Could it possibly be that different things were happening yet causing the same problems? Could it be that we saw the problem only when certain events all happened at the same time. Maybe we just didn't know what to look for. Could it be possible that after more than 35 years in operation we really did not know what made the plant tick? I didn't know the answer, but I knew I had better find it if I expected to keep my job.

The business climate for our product had changed and prices were dropping. More customers were complaining about quality and people were starting to get on each other's nerves. I spoke with our plant president about it the other day, but he said, "don't worry, our business is cyclical and we will get the prices back up soon enough." He always told us our job was to make as much as we could make and the salesmen would find someone to buy it. That was their job. But I just didn't feel good about things. I knew we were falling behind.

4

Economics

Our plant produced catalysts, pigments, and dyes and had been in business for over 35 years. In the beginning, the products were new and everyone wanted them. Not many people knew how to produce them. The first 25 years were good and bad but mostly good. But then things really started to change. More companies had gotten into our business and competition from overseas started bringing prices down. Now our products were commodities, and it seemed everyone made them.

As one old employee told me just after I had started, "You know Barry, I've been here since they started building this place. I've seen everything that has gone on here. Expansions, successes, failures, everything. And the best way I can describe this place is that it makes money in spite of itself."

The problem now was that we were not making money anymore. It didn't take long to see what he meant; the wasted time alone was worth a fortune. And everywhere you looked, there was waste. Perfectly good parts thrown away because it was too much trouble to return them to where they belonged. Someone opens the wrong valve and product goes to the sewer. Off-quality product being made and having to be sold at discount. Batches having to be reworked all the time to get them right. Equipment shutdowns taking longer than expected. New equipment being installed and then reengineered because it didn't work properly. Maintenance having to return two and three times to fix the same problem. And the biggest thing was all the problems that occurred that no one had answers for. It was like the place was haunted sometimes.

A culture had been instilled in our plant and then passed down generation by generation. And I knew that culture was here to stay unless something drastic happened to change it. I just didn't know how to change it.

5

The Visionary

As quality manager, it was my job to handle customer complaints and customer audits. We had received several complaints from one of our customers, Nutech Industries. First we had shipped them the wrong product, and then to compound the problem, the replacement product did not work well.

I knew exactly what had happened. Production had packaged one lot incorrectly and it had slipped through inspection. When Nutech received the product, they found they had a truckload of Yellow 93 pigment and not Yellow 95 pigment. Fortunately they caught the problem. Since we were running low on Yellow 95, we shipped a borderline-quality lot to them and it caused color problems in their formulation. Now their quality manager was coming down to see us and the business was on the line. I knew without being told we could not afford to lose this account.

I received a call from the receptionist that a Mr. Russ Peterson from Nutech was in the lobby to see me. I had met Russ once before but only for a minute. I dropped by the restroom on the way down to check my appearance and headed to the lobby. I had rehearsed my answers last night and was as prepared as I could be. I saw him as I entered the lobby.

"Hello," he said before I had a chance to speak. His voice carried an air of confidence. I was suddenly very nervous as I introduced myself to him.

"Uh, Mr. Peterson, you might not remember me, but I was at your plant in Cleveland a few months ago calling on the purchasing manager with our sales manager."

"I remember you, Barry."

"Great. How was the trip down here?"

"No problems at all. Good connections and a nice change of climate."

"Great, well we are set up in the conference room. So if you will just sign in we will head that way."

We walked to the conference room where we met Jimmy, our VP of sales and Doris, our customer service representative. After introductions and coffee, we all sat down and everyone suddenly looked at me.

I could feel the monkey on my back. "Well, I guess we have some explaining to do Russ," I said trying to appear apologetic.

Jimmy jumped in and said, "We really appreciate your business Russ, and we want to do whatever it takes to keep it."

I thought to myself that we probably shouldn't have sent the wrong product to the customer and then compounded it by sending bad product to replace it if we really appreciated their business, Jimmy.

Russ said, "I really don't care much about what happened in the past. What I need to know is what are you going to do to keep it from happening again?"

I looked at Jimmy and he looked at me. I had this great explanation about a new operator and a malfunction of the lab equipment and the guy didn't even want to hear it.

"Uh, well Russ. We know what happened and we are going to train our people so it does not happen again," I said nervously. This was our basic response to almost every problem it seemed.

"How?"

"*Excuse me*, Russ? How? Well we will train them the right way to do it. Do it right the first time is our goal."

"How?" Russ looked at me and smiled.

I took a deep breath and waved my hands stumped for what to say.

Russ calmly said, "Barry, it is clear to me that HPZ has no real improvement process."

Jimmy jumped in, "Now Russ, we are ISO 9001 certified. We are a quality organization."

Russ looked down and I thought he might start laughing but he simply shook his head and said, "Jimmy, ISO does not mean you know how to fix problems. What I want to know is how you are going to improve. Not just this problem but everything that comes up in the future."

I knew I was in over my head and this guy was no fool, so I asked, "Russ, maybe you can help us out here. To be honest we have tried a lot of things but we still have problems. Do you have some suggestions? We want to improve. We are trying." I looked at Jimmy and I thought he was going to have a stroke.

"Have you ever heard of Six Sigma, Barry?"

"I know what *sigma* is, the symbol for standard deviation."

"Yes, but Six Sigma is an improvement strategy and I have seen it do miraculous things. It is not the answer to everything, but it sure helps."

"We could use some help," I said honestly.

"Question for you, Barry. Do things happen and no one can explain them and then the problem goes away by itself?"

"All the time."

"Do changes in the process help one time but the next time they don't help at all or even make things worse?"

"Yes!" I was starting to get curious.

"Last question." He chuckled.

"Shoot," I said.

"Do your people consider running this plant an art instead of a science?"

I was astonished. "How did you know that? Everyone here says it is an art, not a science. Have you worked in a pigment plant before?"

"No," he was laughing. "But I worked in a lot of plants that thought the same way. At least before Six Sigma."

"But, how do you know so much about us?"

"Barry, most plants that don't have something comparable to Six Sigma in place all answer those questions the same way."

"Really," I answered astonished.

"Really," Russ said.

"So how do we get Six Sigma, and what is it?"

"Let's look at your plant and let me get a feel for things, but I want you to come to Cleveland next week if you are committed to making a change here."

I looked at Jimmy. "Are we committed Jimmy?"

"Absolutely," Jimmy said. Of course Jimmy would have committed to anything if it meant we could keep the business.

"OK. Well let me get you some safety equipment, Russ, and we will go out into the plant. By the way, why do you want me to come next week?"

"Our Blackbelt class is in session so you can see Six Sigma in action."

"You teach your people karate?" I asked skeptically.

"Business self-defense, Barry. To keep your competition from beating you up. You have to see it to understand it."

"If you say so."

After Russ left for the day I told my secretary my travel plans.

"I need to book a flight to Cleveland for next Thursday afternoon, Lori. I want to get in no later than 6 p.m. Get me a rental car. The hotel I will be staying at will be on the fax this afternoon."

"I'll get on it right away. Anything else?"

"Just cancel any appointments I had for Thursday afternoon and Friday."

"I'll take care of it."

On the way home that day I was wondering what this Six Sigma was all about. Could it point us in the right direction? At least it was something. This guy Peterson was certainly different. I wondered what was in it for him. Oh well, never look a gift horse in the mouth. If nothing else, maybe we could at least keep the Nutech business a little longer. Of course, if we didn't change something in the plant, we would lose it eventually. But one thing I had learned early on working at HPZ was to worry about "later" later.

6

Problems, Problems, Problems

I pulled up in front of the building where Pat and Sarah were waiting on me to take them to lunch. We had worked together for a long time and we were all comfortable with each other. Sarah managed the labs and Pat was in charge of the ISO system.

"What kept you so long?" asked Sarah. She got in the front seat and Pat climbed into the back.

"Hey, you're gonna have to give me some more room back here!" Pat shouted as he tried to squeeze in the back seat.

"If you two kids are through arguing, we can go to lunch."

I drove out of the parking lot toward the main road. "What's it going to be for lunch?" No one could ever decide where we should eat.

"I don't want Chinese," said Sarah, "How about Mexican?"

"Mexican is fine with me," I said. "Pat?"

"Mexican's OK by me."

"Mexican it is then."

At the restaurant the waitress brought the chips to the table. "The salsa is pretty hot today," I remarked.

"Good, I like it hot," said Pat.

"Rumor is the plant is going to be sold or shut down. Any truth to that Mr. Quality Manager?" Sarah smiled at me.

"You both know if I was privy to any information, I couldn't say."

"That means it's true, Pat," said Sarah laughing.

"Now I did not say that!" I exclaimed.

"Well?"

"The possibility is always there, that's all I can say. The company wants to stay in this business, but if you owned us, would you keep us?" I looked at both of them.

"I always said this place acts like it just started up, hired a bunch of people off the street, and said 'go figure out how to make something.' You would never believe we have been in operation for over 35 years," Pat replied.

"Well, how are things going in the labs these days and how is the quality Sarah?" I smiled.

"The quality isn't doing any better than the plant. Everyone knows we make our best quality when the plant is running smoothly. Can't you make those guys keep the plant up and running?" She sounded frustrated.

"I'm trying."

"We are getting a lot of requests for resampling and retesting bad product. Some of the retests are coming up good the second time," said Pat.

"How much confidence do we have in our tests?" I asked.

"Everyone I ask says pretty good. They aren't perfect but no test is."

"I guess that's true, but if we retest bad product and it comes out good, what would happen if we retest good product? Would it come out bad?" I wondered out loud.

"We wouldn't ever test good stuff again," Sarah said like I was an idiot. "Sales typically wants us to test and retest until we get a good number so they can have something to ship. As long as we are willing to sign our name to the Certificate of Analysis, they are happy with it."

"I just wonder sometimes how good we are at inspecting our product. I am sure some bad stuff gets by."

"I'm sure of that too. We still get complaints don't we?" Pat kept track of all the complaints.

"Yes, more than enough. Well, there is one thing I can tell you about the company you probably don't know."

"What's that?" Pat and Sarah leaned forward over the table.

"We have a new division president."

"What? When did that happen?"

"This week. New guy named Bob Jones replaced McPeters. I understand McPeters took early retirement, but the rumor mill says he was given the old heave-ho."

"What does that mean for us?"

"It means we have a new captain at the helm. I spoke with Jack, and he's worried because the guy has a reputation for being aggressive. It means we have to solve our profitability problem and quickly." I am sure they heard the panic in my voice.

"Well, Mr. Quality Manager, what is the plan for doing that? Are they going to cut jobs?"

"We need all the people we have, but I am not counting out anything at this point. I am going up to Cleveland on Thursday to meet with a guy I met who might be able to help us. Have either of you ever heard of a program called Six Sigma?"

"Yeah, I read about that in *Quality Progress*," said Sarah. "It's supposed to be the next great quality program to get your plant producing almost zero defects. Remember when we did the Crosby thing and focused on zero defects? This one uses statistics and says you should aim for three parts per million or something like that. Like we have a shot at ever doing that!"

"So it uses a lot of statistics, huh?" I wasn't so sure about the statistics stuff. It typically confused me more than anything else. The engineers that knew some statistics always just argued over what statistics test to use, and I swear they could make the data say anything if they tried hard enough.

"I read it was started by Motorola and now GE and a lot of other big companies are doing it," said Pat.

"GE? Well if they are doing it, there must be something good about it. GE wouldn't undertake something like that if it weren't good. Is it all big companies using it?"

"That's all I know about it," said Sarah.

"Well, I guess we'd better get back to the plant. We've been gone long enough. Hopefully the place hasn't fallen off the face of the earth."

"Wow, you are such a motivational leader Barry," Sarah laughed at me.

"Sorry, I just have a lot to do." I didn't want them to know how serious this was yet. It seemed we were losing money faster every month.

"Thanks for lunch," said Sarah.

"Yeah, thanks for lunch."

"You're welcome. I just hope this guy in Cleveland can point me in the right direction with Six Sigma."

"I don't think quality is our biggest problem, and how will a quality program help us get profitable anyway?" said Pat.

"Good question. But this guy asked me a lot of questions and I swear he has worked in our plant. So if he thinks he knows how to help, I for one am going to listen and listen closely."

"Good luck, Barry."

"Thanks." A little luck never hurt anyone. I sure could use it.

When I got back to the plant, our VP of sales was waiting for me.

"Hi Barry, my friend, my buddy," said Jimmy.

"What do you want Jimmy?" I answered suspiciously.

"Need a little help out of you quality guys."

"What kind of help?"

"I have a customer who wants to buy a bunch of catalyst, 5000 tons to be exact."

"Wow, great! Wait a minute, why are you not smiling?"

"He needs all of it in three months. 2000 tons this month and 1000 a month for three months." Jimmy grimaced but looked hopeful.

"Wow. We have a backlog but we can probably do it. Can he take what we have in the warehouse, some of this off-quality stuff?"

"Uh, that's the other thing. He wants the surface area to be a little tighter than our normal production."

"How much tighter?"

"He wants it to match standard by plus or minus one point."

"You have got to be kidding, Jimmy. We can't do that. We would have to make 10,000 tons to get 5000 tons to meet that specification, and that's if we have no problems."

"He says the competition can do it."

"Well the competition must be better than us then, because we can't do it!"

"So what do I tell the customer?"

"Jimmy, we can't meet that specification. And I doubt the volume is there either right now. They are having all types of mechanical failures in the plant."

"Well, you don't know if you don't try Barry."

"Do you want me to commit to something we can't do and make the customer mad so he never buys from us again Jimmy?"

"Well, just be prepared because corporate knows we were given the chance to get the business."

"What was the price on the 5000 tons?"

"We were going to get 10 cents a pound above our budget."

"You're kidding, Jimmy. If we could make that order, we would make money for the next three months, barring losing any current customers. But there is no way right now. Just cannot be done. I will speak to production about it but don't hold your breath."

"Your call. I will just call the guy and tell him no thanks."

As Jimmy walked out of my office, I felt sick to my stomach. I would definitely be getting a call from Jack. Jack ran the entire plant site and used to be in sales. He was my boss. And once a salesman always a salesman, so Jack stayed in touch with that side of the business very closely.

But if there was one thing I knew, it was what this plant was capable of doing quality-wise. I was fortunate sales didn't just accept the order and *then* tell me about it. They were always doing stupid stuff like that without checking first. It was easy to sell it, but someone had to make it too. We had standard products, but they always promised stuff we could not deliver and then I had to explain that to the customer. Now I had to explain it to upper management too.

I found that I was looking forward to getting on that plane Thursday and spending Friday away from the plant.

7

Cleveland Bound

Wednesday was a big blur. I had gotten the call I had expected from Jack about not being able to meet the big order, and he had me go downtown and explain it to everyone. Those corporate guys had no idea what making catalyst was all about. Everyone says the leadership in a company is what separates the good from the bad companies. No wonder we were in such bad shape.

On the plane, I settled back into my seat and looked out the window. There was an older gentleman sitting next to me working on what looked like some type of legal document. I didn't feel like talking and he didn't look like he wanted to talk, so I stared out the window. My stomach started to growl and I realized I was hungry. I hoped we were going to a good place to eat.

I had time to take a shower after I checked in so I felt better. I was waiting for Russ to meet me in the hotel lobby. I saw him walking in the front door.

"How are you, Barry? Good to see you again."

"Hi, Russ. I sure appreciate you setting up this meeting."

"No problem, we quality professionals have to stick together." He winked and slapped me on the back. "Let's get going, are you hungry?"

"Absolutely! But I am paying."

"I have no problem with that. The restaurant is only a mile or so from here. I think you will like it."

"I am sure I will."

We drove to the restaurant, about a mile down the road on the right. The parking lot was packed. "This is a top-quality establishment, great service, great food, and great atmosphere."

"Works for me."

⸺ ⸺

As we sat down Russ said, "Tell me a little about your background, Barry, and how you came to be in the current situation."

"Well, it's a long story, but I'll give you the short version. I started at HPZ in 1985 as an engineer right out of school. I worked on ways to make the process better."

"I see. So you found a lot of ways to make things better and you made improvements in the plant."

"You know, that's what I think we were supposed to do, but we never seemed to actually improve much. I mean we worked hard, we ran tests, and had a lot of ideas. But when it came right down to really improving things, either we asked for money and did not get it, or we just could not figure out what to do. We tried a lot of stuff, but it didn't seem to work real well. Even when we spent the money, there were always problems starting up a new process and sometimes the old problems were still there. And even worse, a lot of times we had new problems with the new process that were as bad as the ones we were trying to fix."

"How often did you fix something without spending big money?" Russ was taking some notes in a small notebook.

I started chuckling. "It was always spend big money. We had this one engineer, who we always kidded, who could fix anything, except it would cost four million dollars and require four new engineers. We called him four by four. If he didn't get a lot of money he just quit trying to solve the problem."

"So he was able to fix the problems when he got what he wanted?"

"Not really. He always wanted to throw computers and automation and complex equipment at the problem. Then we had stuff we could not maintain. It was typically reengineered out in the plant after he turned it over to production just to keep it running."

"Do you think management would have funded more projects if they had confidence there was a guaranteed payback?"

"Actually, I think we would have asked for more if we had had the confidence that we could have delivered on what we'd promised. Too many of our projects did not deliver the return they were supposed to. I think the bosses got a little scared of getting their hands slapped so we kinda stopped asking."

"One of the things I will show you is how to gain confidence so that upper management works for you, not against you."

"I like that!" I was smiling now.

"OK, so what did you do after that?"

"Well, I moved into a quality role working on quality problems and spent some time doing the Crosby improvement system and ISO and SPC."

"Tell me how those systems changed things at HPZ."

"They really did not have much overall impact. I mean, people were motivated and excited when we were talking about zero defects with Crosby, but it was mainly management. I don't think the shop floor guy really ever got it, and they were not involved much in the program."

"Do you think it is necessary to involve the shop floor workers on improvement ideas, Barry?" Russ was concentrating on me and I could feel his stare.

"I always thought so, but most of our engineers and managers don't think so. To tell you the truth, a lot of people are blaming the production folks for our problems. They say they are screwing things up and not working hard enough."

"Can you believe me when I say the hourly workers and the frontline supervision have to be involved since only these folks know what is really going on? Also, management is responsible for most of the problems because only management can change the things that affect 80 percent of your problems."

"I can buy that, but I doubt the rest of the plant will."

"Good, because it is absolutely true. How about the quality of your products?"

"I think you know the answer to that, Russ."

Russ just smiled.

"We have about a 95 percent on-grade average. Some products are better than others. Of course some tolerances are wide enough to drive a truck through."

"What happens to the 5 percent or so that is off-grade?"

"We either reprocess it or sell it at a discount."

"Barry, do you have any operations before inspection where you check things and reject them?"

"Oh, all over the place. We test hundreds of places. This is a complex process. If it's bad, we reprocess it."

"Don't you consider these in-process rejects as a quality problem?"

"Well, it doesn't get to the customer, so we never really think of it as a problem unless it gets bad enough to slow down the plant."

"We call that the 'hidden factory,' Barry, and it is a potential source of huge improvement in your final product quality, and also in reducing costs."

"We certainly need to reduce our costs."

"OK, what about complaints?"

"We get maybe five a month, not bad."

"Out of how many shipments?"

"Let's see, we will make about 20 truckloads, and 30 days a month is 600 shipments. No wait, some are railcars, so say 500 a month. Yeah, 500 shipments a month."

"And you get five complaints every month. What if I told you only one in 10 customers bothers to actually file a complaint. That means your customers are probably dissatisfied in some way 50 times a month or 10 percent of the time."

"Wow!"

"Now, how many customers do you have in all?"

"Probably 300 or so."

"With 50 complaints a month actually occurring, you probably manage to have problems with most of your customers every year, Barry."

"That's terrible, I thought we weren't doing so bad."

"OK, tell me about this new job you have?"

"A couple of months ago, I became quality manager and they made me a member of the operations team. So I'm in charge of quality now and I guess share responsibility for the whole site with the team. We have been losing money or breaking even for the last five years, and I have been told we must get profitable soon or else. Oh, and we have a new guy running our division and he has a reputation for being a hatchet man."

"So what do you think you need to do to get profitable?"

"Well, a lot of folks want to start laying people off, but we had a big layoff five years ago and people are still mad about that. Labor only accounts for 20 percent of our costs so I could fire everybody and we still would not be profitable."

"That is a common tactic because its easy to do and very short-term. I am glad you see farther than that," Russ replied.

"I know we do a lot of things wrong but the biggest problem is we are so unpredictable. I just turned down a big order at great prices because the customer wanted a product with tighter tolerances and on short notice. I know we can't make it and we have no idea how to make the plant produce it."

"Barry, I will tell you a little secret. All plants are composed of independent variables and dependent variables. We call them Xs and Ys. The Ys are the things you inspect for at the end of each step or the end of the process. It is why you reject those products and send them for rework. Most companies spend most of their time measuring these things so they don't get to the customer. The problem is they are not the reason things go wrong. They depend on the other variables, the Xs, for their response. These X variables are independent of each other and are typically not measured or even known to be important. You have to discover what the X variables in your process are and control them. Then the Y variables will be predictable."

"Are you telling me we are measuring the wrong stuff? We have to inspect the product, don't we? Customers demand that information."

"There is nothing wrong with inspection other than the cost, Barry, but it is not possible to inspect quality into a product. You have to make quality."

"But quality is not where my immediate concern is. It is reducing my costs." I was still confused.

"Remember from Crosby the term PONC or price of non-conformance. It is similar to the COPQ or cost of poor quality."

"That's the price of doing things wrong if I remember back to my Quality College days," I chuckled.

"Exactly, and for most companies, without an active improvement program in place, that cost can exceed 25 percent of your gross sales."

"Wow. That would be like 50 million dollars for us."

"See how the cost comes into the equation. If you under-stand your process, you can predict things and prevent prob-lems from occurring and also take advantage of opportunities like that customer who needed tighter specifications."

"It's starting to make some sense now. How do I do this though?"

"What I have just described to you is the basic approach of Six Sigma. There is a lot more to it that you will see tomorrow."

"So where do we go from here?"

"Come to my office tomorrow at 8:00 a.m. The reception-ist will show you where my office is. We are training our 4th wave of Blackbelts this week and you can talk to some of them. This is their last week of training so you can see some of the projects they are working on. And I will introduce you to Dave, our Six Sigma Master Blackbelt."

"What is the Master Blackbelt?"

"That person is someone who has mastered all of the skills needed to solve complex problems, and can teach them to others. They are worth their weight in gold."

"I can't hardly wait."

We finished our dinner and talked more about Six Sigma. We finally left the restaurant at 11:00 and I was more encouraged than I had been in years. I was starting to think this is just what we needed at HPZ.

8

Six Sigma in Action

I arrived at the Nutech corporate headquarters a few minutes before 8 a.m. and the receptionist pointed me towards Russ's office down the hall.

"Hi, Russ," I said as I poked my head in the door.

"Right on time. I like punctuality." Russ got up and walked over to the door and shook my hand. "Come on in and have a seat."

"Thanks."

"What I have planned today is for you to sit in on the Blackbelt training. I also asked several of the Blackbelts to give you a presentation on their projects. I think you will be impressed."

"Sounds good to me. My flight doesn't leave until 6:30 tonight so I want to learn all I can."

"OK, so let's head down to the conference room."

"Can you answer one question for me before we go?"

"Sure, what do you want to know?"

"Why are you helping me, and how did you learn about Six Sigma?"

Russ smiled and said, "I just like working with people and you remind me of a younger me. You were straight with me about your quality problems. It excites me to see companies improve. The U.S. needs to get on its toes to face the competition. This century is going to be very competitive. So maybe some of it is patriotism, but mostly I just like to work with people who have a passion for making things better."

"Well I really appreciate it. How did you find out about Six Sigma?"

"I got involved with Six Sigma working at Exponex. We had a lot of the same problems you had 10 years ago and Six Sigma helped us out of a lot of them. I left Exponex to come work here, I was getting bored there. Maybe things got too predictable."

"Wow, did you run a plant for them?"

"Kind of, I was responsible for their production operations."

"What location?"

"Worldwide, but we can talk about that later."

"Oh." I had not realized Russ had been such a high-profile person. Exponex was a huge company.

"Let's head down to the conference room." Russ started walking.

As we headed down to the conference room, we chatted about his career and what he was doing for Nutech. We went down in an elevator to the bottom floor and walked into a large conference room. There were rows of tables facing a screen and a big, blond, curly-headed guy was talking to a class of about 30 people. Behind him on the screen was projected a graph of something.

Each of the tables seated three people and everyone had a laptop computer open in front of them and a textbook of some sort.

"Good morning, everyone," said Russ.

"Good morning, Russ."

Most of the class looked up and spoke or acknowledged us as we walked in. It was a very diverse-looking group of people. They seemed to be enjoying themselves.

"I would like to introduce Barry Watson, he works for one of our suppliers, HPZ Chemicals, and he is interested in learning more about Six Sigma."

"Hi," I said to the group, and they welcomed me.

"Barry, this is Dave, he works for Six Sigma Enterprises and he is one of the Master Blackbelts helping us with our training."

"Nice to meet you, Barry," said Dave.

"I'm glad to be here, thanks for letting me interrupt your class."

"Barry, why don't you sit up front here and several of the Blackbelt candidates will tell you about their projects."

"Thanks." I moved up front and sat in an empty seat.

"Denise, would you like to go first?"

"Sure, Dave."

Denise hooked her laptop up to the projector.

"First, welcome to Nutech. My name is Denise and I work in Atlanta at our latex plant. We manufacture latex for the paper industry and my project was to increase our production capacity by 10 percent."

I nodded my head.

Denise continued, "The first step in a Six Sigma project is to form a team of people who know something about what you are trying to solve."

A list of names appeared on the screen.

"These are my team members. We have people from production, maintenance, R&D, and finance." She sounded like a professional speaker.

"Finance?" I questioned.

"Oh yes, if finance doesn't buy into the project and accept the savings, it will never be funded or accepted. All Six Sigma projects are required to have bottom-line impact."

"That is a good idea," I shrugged. It made sense. But our finance folks would get lost inside our plant, I thought. I wasn't sure they had ever actually *been* inside our plant.

Denise continued, "After the team is formed we further develop our problem statement and our goal. As you can see here we want to increase our capacity by 10 percent, which will allow us to make more product with the same number of people and equipment."

"How do you know this is possible?" I could picture me assigning this to my process people and their complaining that it was not possible right off the bat.

"We like to ask how do you know it is not possible? With Six Sigma, we figure out how to solve problems. If we knew how to do it before we started, it would not be a good project for Six Sigma. We would just do it."

"I see, please go ahead. Sorry about the questions, this is all new to me."

"No, please ask questions. We learn from each other also. The next step is to start defining the process. We completely map the process and look for non-value-added steps and data collection points. The operators and mechanics are very valuable here since many times the process is different than what engineering thinks it is. This is the process map."

A block diagram with lines and lists of items appeared.

"What are the Xs and Ys listed there on the map?" I asked.

"Those are the key inputs and outputs of each step as we know it."

"I see." I looked over at Russ and he was nodding his head up and down. This is what he was talking about last night, I thought.

"From here we developed a PFMEA."

"A what?" I asked.

"Sorry. One thing you learn in Six Sigma is a different language; you will pick it up soon. PFMEA stands for process failure mode and effects analysis."

"OK," I said hesitantly.

"The PFMEA breaks down the process into individual little pieces. It then prompts us to assign a ranking to potential failure modes for each piece. And to question the effect those failures will have on our process."

"I see, it sounds like some sort of controlled brainstorming."

"Exactly. We extract the knowledge of the team in a systematic manner. We have to rank each failure mode and effect for three categories: likelihood of occurrence, severity of occurrence, and ability to detect. They all carry equal weight."

"You know, Denise, this sounds a lot like an OSHA HazOp study."

"It is a lot like a HazOp study, Barry. The principles are the same. We want to identify the predominant variables that affect our process just like you are doing for safety in a HazOp."

"OK, let me see if I have it straight so far. The information for the PFMEA comes from the process map and the process map comes from the team, which comes from the people who do the work. Sounds like a good way to get people involved in solving problems."

"You've got it. It can yield a lot of new ideas," Denise said proudly.

Russ added, "This is one of those added benefits of Six Sigma, Barry. In addition to the project savings, it involves people down to the lowest level in the organization. Ultimately, when the organization is really competent in the Six Sigma approach, operators will use it to solve their own problems. They will ask for help from a Blackbelt only if they get stuck."

"Yes, that sounds important to involve everyone in the organization," I added.

Denise continued with her presentation. "The next step is to validate your measurement systems. We take measurements after reaction and before shipments for a number of quality checks. If we did not pass them after reaction, we extended the reaction and checked them again. If we still did not pass, we had to reprocess or sewer depending on how bad it was. We also measured our defects per million opportunities and calculated a baseline sigma score."

"The sigma is kind of like process capability, right?" I asked.

"Yes it is. To check our measurement systems, we ran gage R&R studies on all of the test methods we were collecting data from."

"I thought R&R stood for rest and relaxation," I said puzzled. Everyone laughed.

Denise responded, " No actually R&R stands for repeatability and reproducibility. And it is not very relaxing either."

The group laughed again. Everyone here seemed to be so into the training. Not like training classes I had been to.

"So it tells you if your test is any good?"

"Yes, Barry, there is a standard method in our software package for conducting the studies, and we found that some of our tests were not able to measure accurately what we were trying to measure. This helped us make some test changes and we dropped some tests because they were so inaccurate; they just held up production."

"Let me get this straight, you had tests that were holding up production and they were not even accurate?"

"That's right."

"How long had you been running these tests?" This interested me.

"For 20 years." Denise was proud of her accomplishments.

"That's amazing." I thought about the tests we had run for 35 years.

Dave added, "This is a common problem we run into all the time. It is especially critical when you run experiments and you have to have accurate data."

Denise continued, "After we validated all the tests and made changes as needed to replace the bad ones, we went into the analysis mode. Our process map and the PFMEA had pointed out a lot of potential problems, more than we could begin to study at one time. Everything clear so far?"

"Kind of, but go on, it is making more sense."

"To help decide which ones to study further, we analyzed all of our data using techniques like multiple regression, scatter plots, histograms, and analysis of variance. Then we were able to predict the critical variables."

"Those statistical tests are pretty complicated aren't they, Denise? I mean you need a PhD in statistics to use that stuff right?"

"Barry, we all thought the same thing before we went through the training. But the way it is taught, with real-life examples and lots of practice . . . it just made sense to me.

I had been through classes in statistics before, but this is the first time it really seemed to stick."

"Wow, that is great," I said. "We seem to send someone to a class every year involving some kind of statistics but it never seems to become part of our culture."

"I know what you mean, Barry. I would have said the same thing before we started Six Sigma. But using what we learned about statistics we were able to whittle down the potential areas of study to: the amount of time we spent in reaction, the wait time between batches, and the number of batches we had to reprocess."

"That's impressive, Denise." I meant it too.

"But now we needed to further break down our process and really study each part. We do that in the *improve* phase. This is where we start to model the process and actually find ways to predict the behavior. This is the exciting part and here is how we do it."

Denise showed a slide on the screen.

"You lost me, Denise." The slide showed what looked like a matrix of numbers and statistics I could not comprehend.

"Well, it really only looks complicated. We randomly vary the critical factors in a high and low level and determine the effect on the output. The computer does all of the work for you. The statistics tell you what is significant and what is not. It's called a DOE or design of experiments."

"I'll have to study that some, but it works?"

"It is the most efficient way to perform experiments and you actually can learn how factors influence each other in ways that you cannot learn by changing one factor at a time."

"What did you learn from your experiments?"

"Well, I'll keep it simple for you for now. Once you go through Blackbelt training it is easy to understand. These were the reactor variables we came up with using our define and analysis tools: pressure, temperature, amount of defoamer, and concentration. The response was reaction time to completion."

"Are these all the variables that affect the reactor time, Denise?"

"Oh gosh no, Barry. There are dozens more. This is the reason the analysis phase tools help so much. So we can pick out the critical variables that have the best chance to help us make the process do what we want it to do."

"I'm starting to get it now, Denise. At our plant, we think our processes are so complex we will never control them and what you are saying is that most of the variables don't make that much difference, only a few have a lot of impact."

Dave added, "You have hit the nail on the head, Barry. The secret is to be able to identify the variables that have the biggest contribution to the response *before* you start running experiments. You simply cannot run experiments with large numbers of variables. They take too long, cost too much, and there is too much to try and control."

Denise continued, "Dave is right. Because we only had to manipulate four things it worked great, and what we found was totally unexpected. If we increased the pressure but lowered the temperature, the reaction was complete in less time but only if we left the defoamer out. Plus the concentration made no difference at all."

"Did you control those factors before, Denise?" I asked.

"Not really. We had a recipe we had been doing for 20 years and everyone said you had to do it that way. I found out you didn't. It surprised everyone at the plant."

"Did anyone disagree with you?"

"Actually, quite a few people were skeptical, but Dave came in and reviewed my data. We then ran a follow up DOE and validated my conclusions. It really does work. The funniest part is, a lot of the research folks were absolutely sure concentration was critical and we found it didn't even matter. We used to hold up a lot of batches just to get the concentration right."

"That's amazing."

Denise was beaming. "The best part was, the operator was the one who said the defoamer was hurting us, but no one would listen to him. He said they ran out of defoamer a couple of times in the past but we kept running anyway. He noticed the reaction was faster without it. Plus the defoamer is expensive so we can save some money not using it. Maybe we used to need it, but our raw materials are better or something because we sure don't need it now. "

"So the operator was the one who had the answer?" That was interesting, I thought. We had a lot of people who thought the operators were stupid just because they didn't have college degrees.

Denise chuckled. "Yes, he just didn't know he had a good idea. When he first noticed it, he told a couple of people who didn't listen to him because he was just an operator, so he let it drop. Other people convinced him he was wrong. When we made him part of the team, we learned from him what was really happening. Without Six Sigma and the operator on the team, we never would have thought to look at that defoamer variable."

"I like that story. Can I tell my folks back at HPZ about it?"

"Sure, tell anybody you want but our competition." Denise smiled and continued. "What we are learning this week is how to perform advanced experimental designs to optimize the process. I intend to do a steepest-ascent run next week to find the optimum conditions to get the fastest reaction time. With Six Sigma, you keep improving until you have a process that is robust enough where you don't have to worry about it."

"Well, did you meet your initial goal of a 10 percent reduction?" I asked.

Denise laughed again. "That is the best part. Here is what I learned in the four months I have been doing this Six Sigma project. We were holding up batches for two and three hours waiting for lab results that didn't tell us anything, so we eliminated that test. We then found that we could save money by lowering the temperature and leaving out the defoamer if we increased the pressure. We also completed the batches 25 percent faster that way. And last of all we eliminated unnecessarily adjusting 10 percent of the batches for concentration. When you add it all up, we will save $150,000 in defoamer and steam costs and reduce the overall batch cycle time by 30 percent. This means we will be able to make 15 percent more product for less money and go out and get new business. The value of that new business is conservatively estimated at 1.2 million dollars annual profit since we won't have to increase our fixed costs. We also don't have to invest between 20 and 30 million dollars of capital to get that amount of productivity gain."

I looked over at Russ and he smiled at me. All I could do was shake my head and stare at Denise.

"OK, who is next?" Dave asked.

"Well mine is not quite so dramatic as Denise's project but it will save us about a quarter million dollars a year," said Chris.

"I can't wait to hear about it."

"My project involves making wallpaper. We manufacture wallpaper at our plant in Alabama, and my project was to reduce the waste involved. Theoretically, we were losing about 3 percent of our total output through scrap and other sources, based on raw material consumption. We went through the same process as Denise, of course.

Russ added, "The nice thing about Six Sigma is you follow a proven methodology and the tools work for almost anything."

Chris continued, "Here is the process map and the PFMEA. You can see we identified three or four opportunities, but the PFMEA also identified one we had not thought of. We sell wallpaper by the roll and we didn't know how accurate we were in getting the proper yardage on the roll. We really didn't think it was a problem, but because we didn't know, it ranked pretty high on the PFMEA.

"I need to learn more about this PFMEA, Russ."

"You will," he replied.

"We started looking at scrap first, and found out we recycled most of the scrap; when we started measuring what actually we threw away it was not that much. We do sell a lot of seconds, but that was not the focus of this project."

Dave added, "You tend to generate a lot of spin-off projects also, Barry. Like the amount of seconds sold at a reduced price.

Since it was not being scrapped it was not showing up as a defect on the books. The next Blackbelt wave will work on reducing the seconds produced."

"So we finally turned to looking at the amount on each roll. We really had not thought that was a problem at first because we do measure it, but we followed the Six Sigma approach and it worked. What we found was that most of our rolls had between 2 percent and 4 percent too much wallpaper."

"Really." I wondered how much our bags of product really had in them.

"The worst part was, we knew it. It had been a part of the process for years to add a little extra to make sure the customer did not complain. One of our old-timers said they had some complaints 20 years ago about short rolls, but that was when we had the old measuring equipment so short might have been a foot short. So they just added a little extra to be sure."

"This is a common problem," said Dave. "I see it all the time. People make changes to correct a problem but they really just attack the symptom without identifying the source of the problem. Sometimes the problem goes away or the process changes, but the correction stays in place and then just chews up resources. No one questions it because it just becomes part of the way we do business after a certain amount of time."

"That's exactly right, Dave. We installed accurate measuring equipment five years ago and we can control to the inch. Everyone believed it was a requirement to add more. When sales asked our major customers if an inch too much or too little would make a difference to them, they said no, so we placed the tolerance right on the label, and now we make more rolls, and it added up to a quarter million dollars in sales we were giving away."

"What did the folks say who worked in the plant?"

"They knew we added a little extra but they had no idea it was worth that much. They thought we had to do it to meet some customer requirement. Even the plant manager thought it was a customer requirement."

"So the problem does not have to be complex to apply the Six Sigma approach?"

"Absolutely not," said Russ. "Some of the biggest improvements I have seen have been simple fixes."

"That is amazing."

"In addition Barry, you can see from Denise's project she incorporated some lean manufacturing concepts into her project. We teach lean as a part of our Six Sigma process as well," informed Dave.

"Well, any further questions for these two, Barry?" said Russ.

"I am just overwhelmed right now with possibilities for my plant. I need to know how to get my people trained to work like this. This could really make a difference in our plant. I am sure we have tons of opportunities."

Russ laughed, "Now don't think we get this kind of savings on every project. These two are really extra special but similar cases exist in most plants. On average a Blackbelt project will save 75,000 dollars a year and take three to six months to complete. Of course a Blackbelt can work on several projects at a time so the savings add up. And the best part is, once you fix the root cause and understand the X variables, the savings are there every year."

"I have a feeling we have some real biggies in our plant."

"I hope you do. Dave will spend some time with you during lunch on what it takes to get a program off the ground. I have to head up to a meeting so I will come back down in a few hours."

"Thanks for all the help, Russ." He was already headed out of the room.

"Ready to hear a couple more projects, Barry?" said Dave.

"Can't wait."

"OK, Tim, why don't you go. Yours is interesting. He has a finance project. We call it a transactional project. Something that involves transactions instead of manufacturing."

"The Six Sigma approach works for things other than plant problems?"

"Well, Barry, everything we do is actually a process, but if you mean nonmanufacturing, sure it does. Actually if you listed all the things done in your plant, you would have more nonmanufacturing processes than manufacturing processes. Think about all the decisions made, the paperwork, the orders, the bill payments. And on and on and on."

"Well, I suppose you are right there."

"Today Six Sigma is being applied to financial institutions, healthcare, insurance, service industries, and everything in between."

"Wow. It really is a growing trend then."

"Things that work tend to do that," Dave smiled.

I sat back and listened to two more projects. I wondered what would have happened if we had done this type of stuff back on my first project in 1985 and if that test would have been successful. I know I would have been more confident in my abilities if I had been a Blackbelt back then.

The thought of all the time I had wasted in the last 15 years working on things that might have been solved made me feel a little sick. I was more convinced than ever that we had to start this as soon as I got back home. We were still using new people as only a pair of hands where they could be out solving real problems with these types of tools.

Dave and I sat over in the corner at lunchtime.

"Tell me what is involved in starting a Six Sigma program, Dave."

Dave said, "First of all, it really is not a program. A program has a start and a finish. Six Sigma is really a way of doing business, and it never ends."

Dave continued, "The first step is to gain upper management commitment. It really will not work without it. It works best if the CEO or the highest official becomes a PR person for Six Sigma."

I listened intently.

"Once you have the top guy's support, we do an executive training course teaching the basics to top management. We then do champion training. Champions are managers who will have Blackbelts working with them or for them. They have to understand what is going on and also support it. Each Blackbelt will have a champion."

"The Blackbelts don't work for Russ?"

"No, not really. He has them during training, but they work for their champions, typically their current boss or the boss of the area that their project is assigned in."

"I see why the champion is so important now."

"Right, the champion helps select the project. They break down roadblocks and support the Blackbelt. They review the project every step of the way and offer moral support too. This is really hard work, and it is stressful. These are high-profile projects. There is always the fear of failure."

"What do you mean failure?"

"A Blackbelt has to complete their projects to be certified. If the goal is not met, they don't get certified. They have to show they have grasp of all the tools we teach them, also."

"Wow, that is a lot of pressure. Do many people fail?"

"Some do, but those are usually people that just don't work at it. They will succeed if they work diligently, and we make sure the projects they work on during the training phase are achievable. Project selection is critical. People can work on more complex projects once they have mastered the tools."

"How much training is required, Dave?"

"There are typically four weeks of training, with each training week separated by three weeks of project work. We also support the Blackbelts at their plant sites in between training sessions. Of course, Blackbelts from previous training sessions can help also. The first week covers *define* and *measurement*, the second week is *analysis*, the third week is *improvement*, and the fourth week is *control*. We call it DMAIC for short."

"So let me see. I'm starting to understand Denise's project better now. 'Define and measurement' is the problem statement and team formation, test validation and mapping, and PFMEA. What is 'analysis' week?"

"Analysis is when they use statistics to analyze data that is currently available. We teach things like confidence limits, multivariate analysis, analysis of variance, and all types of basic and advanced stats. Everything you need to make good decisions from data."

"I certainly see a need for that. When we look at data, everyone argues over what it means. It gets pretty ugly at times. Everyone wants to find a statistic that makes the data fit their ideas. If it doesn't they blame statistics as worthless."

"I have seen that too. Statistics take the 'gut feeling' out of decision making so the data speaks for itself. We teach the proper test for the proper data. But more important is, you have to have good data. Remember the bad test?"

"Oh yeah, the bad test data. And then 'improve' has to be the DOE stuff Denise talked about."

"Basically that is right."

"And what about 'control'?"

"We teach SPC, control charts, control plans, and advanced topics."

"I wondered if control charts were something you taught. We have tried them but it just does not seem to help."

"Well, Barry, what are you charting and how good is your measurement? If you have not identified the critical X factors, you don't know what to control so a control chart won't help you improve. And if your measurement is no good, well . . . ."

"That explains it. We usually chart the Y variable, I guess. When it goes out of control we don't know what to do anyway so the charts are just ignored or the limits are so wide they are worthless."

"You have to remember, Barry, control charts only tell you when your process is not behaving normally. They do not tell you what to do, only when you should do something. Six Sigma will help you understand what to do."

"We certainly need to know what to do, that's for sure. How much does it cost? Could your company do our training?"

"We might be able to, I will have to check with my partners. I am finished here in a few weeks, but they may have scheduled something I do not know about. As far as cost, it depends on the number of people and the number of waves and how much site support you need."

"Can you give me a ballpark estimate, say for 20 people?"

"The cost differs by company and other factors like class size and travel time, but with one day of support per person you can estimate around $25,000 per person. That includes the executive training, champion training, books and such, too."

My eyes opened wide, "That's over half a million dollars for twenty people. I had no idea it would be so expensive."

"Look at it this way. It is an investment in your people. We guarantee you will recoup your investment if you let us help select the projects that are worked on. You can't lose. There are people who may do it cheaper but you get what you pay for."

"I guess you are right. Half a million to save my plant and save millions in the long run really isn't that much. You said something about us training our own people. How does that work?"

"You can purchase our training materials, and we let you use them after we are gone. You need to do like Russ is doing and develop at least one Master Blackbelt who can do the training. Russ is training one for each division. Russ chooses people who have done exceptionally well as a Blackbelt, and we can help you decide who is well suited. Denise, for example, will probably end up being a Master Blackbelt for her division."

"I can certainly see why he would choose Denise."

"You will have a few folks who end up being really good at this and also have the people skills. Master Blackbelts also work on big systemwide problems."

"Could you come down and help me explain it to our upper management?" I was going to need some help selling this approach. I hoped Jack would be able to see the big picture and not just the money.

"Sure, just give me some notice."

"I will after I get my boss's initial reaction. I am convinced we need to do this. I just hope I can convince upper management of it." The amount of money worried me. I had to figure out a way to get them to buy in on this. I just had to.

"OK, call me and we will schedule it, Barry."

"Thanks, Dave. I will."

9

The Big Sell

I spent the rest of the day in Cleveland talking to the Blackbelts, and since Russ was tied up, we only had a few minutes to talk before I had to leave for the airport. I told him I was concerned about the cost of the program when we were losing money, and he said if upper management could not see the potential in Six Sigma, they probably would not support it even if it were free.

He told me Exponex found out that training costs had one of the biggest returns on investment (ROI) of anything they had ever invested in. GE was finding out the same thing and was increasing their efforts to train more people. At Nutech, their returns on just the projects done during training were more than paying for the cost of training, even including the trainee's salary.

Russ offered to come see us and I told him I might take him up on his offer. The last thing Russ warned me about was placing all the emphasis on Six Sigma. He explained that there were many critical parts to running a successful business and Six Sigma would help many of them, but it was not a silver bullet.

If you made products no one wanted, Six Sigma could not help even if they were the best quality in the world. I laughed when he said there was not much of a market these days for low-cost high-quality 8-track tape players.

I told him I was worried most about reducing the costs in my plant right now. We both felt Six Sigma could do that, but first I had to gain Jack's support.

I called Jack when I got back in the plant on Monday. "Hi Jack, this is Barry."

"Hi, Barry, where were you on Friday? I tried to get you but your secretary said you were out of town on business. Any problems?"

"No, not really, but that was kind of what I was calling you about."

"Well, what's cooking?"

"Actually I need to see you in person about something."

The phone went silent for a few seconds. "You aren't going to quit on me are you?" said Jack hesitantly.

"No, no—nothing like that. I just need to go over something with you. It's very important."

"Well, I can make some time this afternoon. How about 2:00? No, tell you what, come on over at noon and I'll buy you lunch."

"Noon is fine. I'll see you at headquarters."

"You're sure you aren't going to quit on me?" said Jack.

"No, Jack, but thanks for caring."

As soon as I hung up the phone, it rang. It was Jimmy.

"Barry, we have a problem and I need it taken care of today." He sounded like he was out of breath.

"OK, Jimmy, what's the problem?" Everything was a disaster to Jimmy. He always tended to overreact.

"You know that account we have up in New York, the paper mill."

"You mean Margon?"

"Yes, we are sole supplier and we are about to shut them down. You guys haven't made a pound of P-101 in-spec in weeks. What are you going to do about it? I have to call them back in 10 minutes and give them an answer."

"Jimmy, we have made plenty of P-101 recently so we must have some in inventory. We make the stuff all the time and I don't recall seeing any off-grade produced. I can't give you any answers in 10 minutes. Why didn't you say something weeks ago."

"We put the orders on schedule and you are supposed to meet them," Jimmy said sarcastically.

"I know that Jimmy, but a little heads-up before we shut a customer down would help me next time, OK?"

"OK. Just get me an answer of when we can ship. This company cannot afford to lose this account as bad as things are. You know the competition is breathing down our necks. I do not need these kinds of quality problems, Barry."

"I will call you back as soon as I know something, Jimmy." I felt like slamming the phone down but I didn't.

I called Sarah first to see why we didn't have material to ship on-grade for Margon Specialty Paper. We had been selling to them for years with no problems that I could remember. I had even been to their plant a couple of times in my role as quality manager, and the product was always working fine when I was there.

"Sarah speaking."

"Hi, guess who?"

"What do you want?"

"Margon? What's the story?"

"So Jimmy called you? I figured he would. The basic story is we haven't been making product to meet their spec and the plant can't find out why."

"What do you mean?" I said incredibly. "We have supplied them for years. We never had this problem before." It made no sense to me and I was getting fed up with all the problems we had been having.

"Well, about two months ago, they had some type of discoloration problem they thought was caused by the pigment. Billy from technical service went up to investigate and the next thing I know Billy set a specification on the conductivity of P-101 for them at 16 plus or minus 0.2."

"Why did he do that?"

"He looked at the shipment data and thought the problem might be caused by the conductivity, so he convinced them this spec would fix the problem. I think he just told them that so he could say he did something."

"You have got to be kidding me. We can't control to that level."

"I know, but that is right in the middle of our target range and we usually have most of our product come out there so we figured we would just lot-select stuff for them. We make a lot of P-101 anyway, and they buy a small amount of it so we didn't think it would be a problem. Maybe I shouldn't have agreed to it?"

"Well the customer specs are the responsibility of sales, but this one sounds like we screwed ourselves. So what is the production problem?"

"For the last two weeks the conductivity has been low, on everything. I informed Lou in production, and he said they were trying to make adjustments but so far it has not changed. It's just coming out low."

"Let me call Lou. Thanks Sarah." I hung up and called Lou.

"Hello, production department, Lou speaking."

"Lou, this is Barry."

"What's up?"

"Tell me about the P-101 conductivity problem."

"Oh yeah, I meant to tell you about that. We have been putting out so many fires, it slipped my mind."

"Yeah right, what's happening?"

"The problem is, sales set another tight spec without asking us and we can't meet it now. Go blame those guys."

"I know about the spec and I will take it up with Jimmy, but we used to make plenty of product in that spec range."

"Well, we don't now."

"Why not?"

"We don't know."

"What are you doing about it?"

"Well, James sent a bunch of samples up to lab for testing and we made a small change on the pump settings but so far it hasn't helped."

"So why aren't we doing something else?"

"We have to see if this is going to fix it first. I can't go out and just start changing a bunch of stuff at the same time. We won't know what fixed it if we change more than one thing at a time."

"In the meantime, Lou, we are going to shut this customer down and they are a good customer. We can't afford to lose them."

"I don't know what to tell you, we are doing all we can. Why don't you get some of those engineers up in R&D to get out of their offices and help us out? You never see those guys out here when we have problems."

"I am sure they have their own problems to fix Lou, but if you need the help I will certainly give Mark a call."

"Never mind, those guys in R&D are useless anyway for the most part. Half of them don't even know anything because they are so new. It takes years of working in this plant to know how to make pigment."

"I know Lou, this is an art, not a science." I just shook my head as I said it.

"We'll try and speed things up, Barry."

"We're getting ourselves in a hole we will never be able to climb out of."

"I'll do everything I know how to do."

I hung up the phone with Lou and glared out the window. This place was ridiculous. Why did sales agree to something with a customer without knowing what caused the problem? A discoloration problem in a paper mill could be caused by a number of things. It probably wasn't even the pigment. Now we had this specification around our necks like a noose and once those things are agreed to, it's chiseled in stone.

And worse, now the plant can't make what it has made for years. That's an old story. What do our guys do? Take samples and make insignificant changes and say they are doing all they know how to do. That's when it hit me like a rock between the eyes. That was all they knew how to do? It really was.

That was the problem. That *was* all they knew how to do! I thought back to my early years just out of school. They didn't teach us stuff at school like Denise was doing up at Nutech. Sure I had statistics, but it was never taught in a way that made sense in a real-world setting.

When I came to work here, I learned to solve problems just like Lou was trying to with this problem. Add to that the fact that everyone believed it was supposed to be this way since it was an art and not a science. No wonder we were going out of business.

What if our competition used tools like Six Sigma to run their plant? We were doomed to failure if we did not change something. Sales blamed production for not making product in specification. Production blamed sales for selling what we could not make. We had to break that cycle.

— —

I pulled up alongside Jack's parking spot at the headquarters building. He was driving another new company car. That was a sore spot with the plant workers. The executive team all had company cars and they replaced them every few years, and some seemed to change every year. We had plant equipment that was 40 years old but a fleet of new cars for our execs. What was wrong with this picture? I explained to my people that rank has its privilege. It still came up every time I talked about cost cutting. It was hard to defend.

I rode the elevator up to the second floor where our company had the entire floor. I walked down to Jack's secretary.

"Hi, Tamara, I'm here to meet Jack for lunch."

"Just go in, Barry."

I walked in the door and Jack was on the phone. He motioned me to sit.

"I don't care what you have to do, that order gets shipped on time. Just make it happen, OK?" He hung up the phone.

"Problems?" I asked.

"It's always something, isn't it. Why can't things just go as planned. Customer orders it, we make it, we sell it, customer pays us, and we make more. Is it so difficult?"

I thought to myself, that is a great introduction to my Six Sigma sales presentation.

"OK, hotshot, what is so important you could not tell me on the phone?" Jack said impatiently.

I decided to just tell it like I saw it. "I have found something I think will make us profitable, something that will help us understand our plant, and also make us a more quality-oriented producer."

"Sounds great, did you steal the plans from our competition?"

"No, I spent the day with a customer of ours. Russ Peterson at Nutech." I braced myself for his response.

"Why are you visiting customers? I need you in the plant getting product out the door," Jack said, sounding upset.

"I was there to look at an improvement program, well not a program, but a different way to make your plant better." I found myself starting to sweat. It was kind of hard to explain what Six Sigma was really all about.

"Isn't Nutech the people we sent the wrong product to?"

"Yes, but that's not the point. The point is they have a new person who came from Exponex and he brought an approach called Six Sigma with him and they are doing unbelievable things with it."

"I heard of that Six Sigma stuff from TechMotion. They tried to push that stuff on our electronics division. Something about three defects in a million is all they will allow or they will not buy from you."

I replied, "Well I don't know about that. Six Sigma is about reducing defects to low levels, but it is more about how to do it, not just a number. As an example, Nutech just found out that in their latex plant they have 30 percent more production capacity than they thought."

"Really, 30 percent more, it must have been overdesigned to start with."

"No, they found out that several things, including the conditions they used to make latex, could be improved and their cycle time was cut by 30 percent. They are after new business now to fill up the plant."

"That's interesting, Barry, but latex production is pretty simple, pigment production is a lot more complex than that. Just because it works there doesn't mean it will work with pigment. Everyone says making pigment is tougher than most things."

"Jack, I think it's tough because we don't understand what makes it work, and everybody thinks they have something unique or harder than anyone else."

"Barry, we have been making pigment forever at that plant, we have to know everything there is to know after 35 years. Come on, give me a break."

"I am telling you, Jack, we don't know what it takes to make it right. We cannot predict what will come out at the end of the process." I was trying to keep my cool.

"Come on, Barry, it's not that bad."

"Yes, it is, Jack. We had to turn down 5000 tons of business the other day because we don't know how to make pigment with the characteristics the customer wanted. That's your idea of being an expert at making pigment?" I was starting to get mad, which I knew was a bad thing to do when you were trying to sell something, especially to a former salesman.

"Listen, Barry, making pigment is different than making the stuff this Nutech plant makes. And Motorola and GE are making light bulbs and assembly-line stuff. It's not the same. Pigment is basically chemical processing."

"Latex is chemical processing too, Jack. It's all the same. We just think we are different. It's only because we don't know the critical X factors of our process."

"Our what? X-files? Well I can see someone worked a number on you with this stuff. What do we have to do anyway? And why would a customer with a complaint want to help us?"

"I don't have all the answers yet, but from what I have read and what I saw at Nutech, it is not complex, really. We take some of our best people and train them using the Six Sigma methodologies and assign them projects to complete. A lot of companies achieve tremendous breakthroughs like the latex plant did."

"Barry, we are shorthanded as it is and I am sure not about to go out and hire people when we are losing money. Plus we need our best people doing what they are already doing."

"You don't have to hire anyone Jack." I threw up my hands. "We have all the people we need. They are already trying to find the answers; they just are not very good at it. Six Sigma will make them better."

"OK, so what if I buy that we don't need more people? Who does their job while they get this training?" he said with a shrug.

"Other people. We do so much stuff we don't need to, and what is more important than understanding what makes our plant operate correctly anyway?" I glared back.

"What do we need to do, send someone off to learn this stuff?"

"No, it requires a lot more commitment than that. I want to train 20 people and start as soon as possible."

"20 people? That sounds like a lot, Barry."

"That is actually just the beginning. Ultimately we should plan on some type of training for everyone in the organization. Different levels for different jobs. We need all the help we can get if we want to turn this place around."

"Sounds pretty ambitious."

"Not really."

"Who does this training? This guy at Nutech?"

"No, we have to bring in outside folks to do the training."

Jack gave me the look. "You mean consultants," he said. "You know how I feel about consultants."

"I know we have had some bad experiences, but these guys are trainers. Once they train us, we can train our own people from then on out."

"What's it going to cost us?"

I was dreading this question. "It will cost us about $25,000 per person." I sat back in my chair and waited on what I knew was coming.

Jack opened his eyes wide, "$25,000 times 20 people. That's half a million dollars. What are you teaching these folks, how to turn pigment into gold?"

"Actually it is more like finding the gold that is already in our pigment plant. I know it sounds like a lot of money, but they will guarantee we recoup our training investment back in two years. I know we can pay it off with the things we find wrong in the plant. Plus it is an investment in our people. That is one of our core values, remember, training and people development."

"Yeah, but half a million dollars. Tell you what. Leave the stuff for me to read. I would have to clear this through my new boss anyway. No way I'm sticking my neck out that far without his approval."

"Jack, this is good stuff. I have worked in this plant 15 years trying to make it better and so have dozens of others. Basically, it is the same place as it was 35 years ago. I just know there are some innovative solutions and ideas that will get us competitive again. We need to show our people how to tap into how the plant operates. Promise me you will talk to this new guy Bob Jones soon."

"He is coming in Wednesday to look us over and he wants to see the plant, too. I will discuss it with him and let you know what he says."

"Great, I really appreciate it."

"OK, let's go get some lunch. I'm starving. So this plant found 30 percent extra capacity?"

"That's what they showed me."

"Hey, make sure the plant is clean for Wednesday too. We need to make a good impression on this new guy."

"I'll talk to Charlie about cleaning things up."

10

The Leader

After lunch, I was feeling better about my conversations with Jack. I needed to call Dave back and see if he could come down and talk to us. The sooner the better as far as I was concerned. I had a nice relaxing lunch with Jack and I actually found myself forgetting about work for a while. The more we talked the better I felt that Jack was getting the big picture. The biggest problem I had with Jack and most of the VPs was the fact that they had never actually worked in manufacturing. They had no feel for what it took to get the product made correctly and out the door on time.

They were smart people, I was sure of that, but you needed some shop floor experience to understand what Six Sigma is really about, which is people. You need to maximize the creativity and energy of your workers. Shop floor workers might not know *why* things happen, but they know *what* happens. I was feeling sure Jack was getting the picture. He had even quit complaining about the money. He promised to talk to his new boss as soon as possible about Six Sigma.

I got my first look at our new division president, Robert Jones, early Wednesday when he and Jack arrived in Jack's new company car. I would hear about Jack's new vehicle before the day was out, I was sure. Jack had his own parking place with his name on it at the plant even though he spent very little time here. It was the closest parking place to the main building and everyone could see it. People would know. Believe me they would know. The stupid paper dealer tag was still on the car.

Robert, or Bob, as Jack said he liked to be called, was tall and slim. I watched him walk into the main building where Jack had a second office. I wondered if Jack had spoken to him yet about Six Sigma. I was not going to be able to meet with Bob one-on-one until after lunch. All of the managers were scheduled to meet in the big conference room to hear the state of the business. I hurried to my office to check on things before the big meeting.

I squeezed in the conference room about one minute after the hour. There were some things I had to take care of that morning and I had lost track of time. The conference room was full and most of the seats were taken so I stood in the back against the wall with Pat and Sarah.

"Has he started yet?" I asked Pat.

"He just walked around and shook hands. Seems like a good guy."

"Well that's good."

Jack walked up to the front of the room and looked like he was ready to get started. The room got quiet.

"Thanks for everyone taking time out of their busy day to come over this morning. For those who have not met him yet, this is our new division president, Robert Jones."

"Please call me Bob," said our new boss.

"With that, I will let Bob take over and tell you about himself and what he has in store for our division." Jack accentuated the word Bob to let everyone know he could follow directions.

"Thanks, Jack, I do not have a prepared speech today. It's way too early in our relationship to bore you with one of those." He laughed and people chuckled. At least he had a sense of humor.

"I will tell you a little about myself. I am a chemical engineer by education but I have worked in process operations, marketing, and management during my career. I recently left Calastar to take this job and I am very happy to be here."

Well, I thought to myself, some operations experience. Good.

Bob went down a list of about a dozen topics and I watched Jack's reaction. He had obviously not heard this before.

"Now this is a pet peeve of mine. I have seen your expenses and you seem to use a lot of consultants. We need to do more things with our own people," Bob said.

I thought Jack was going to sink into the floor. We had made a decision in 1999 to put in a plantwide computer system to try and get everything we did into one computer database. We had an old system that was not Y2K-compliant and we needed something better. The problem was it took longer to implement than expected and we needed a lot of consultants to get it done. It went way over budget.

Then it hit me. Oh no! Jack will never try to sell Bob on Six Sigma now because of Bob's comments on consultants. But Six Sigma people were not consultants; they were trainers, I wanted to scream at Jack.

I looked at Jack and his eyes met mine for an instant and then he looked away. I did not hear anything else Bob said the rest of that day.

My meeting with Bob got canceled. He called to say he would get with me on his next trip. He had to spend some more time in finance trying to make heads or tails out of our costs. Obviously, profitability was what he had been brought in to do. I wished him luck and said for him to call me if he had any questions.

—⁓

I called Jack on Thursday. "Good morning, Jack."

"Good morning, Barry."

"How did the visit go with Bob. I want to tell my folks something."

"Oh, he didn't have any problems with the way things looked except for the books. How are all those cost-cutting project ideas coming?"

"We are still trying to get some of the ideas implemented but so many of them require capital and are long-term projects." It never failed that when the market turned sour and we started losing money, upper management started asking for cost-cutting ideas. I guess it never occurred to them to improve our costs when we actually had money to spend. The guys in the plant usually just pulled out their files and changed the date on the ideas they submitted the last time they were asked for ways to cut costs, since they never seemed to get done.

I was even tempted one year to suggest we change our vision statement to "More, better, faster, cheaper." That really summed it up but I didn't have the nerve to turn it in.

"Well we'd better get something and soon; this guy is no beat-around-the-bush kind of guy. He is going to takes names and kick butt. I've seen his type before." Jack sounded scared.

"Well, maybe we need a swift kick in the butt to get us moving."

"That's what you say now. Don't forget you're top management now too," Jack said warning me.

"Well, how about Six Sigma. You said you had to clear it with Bob and I need to set things up with Dave as soon as possible. That will get us moving in the right direction."

"Well, we may have a problem there," Jack said.

I got real quiet. "You said you agreed to it, Jack, and would back it during lunch the other day."

"It's not me, Barry. I brought it up with Bob and he just could not see paying consultants more money right now. Especially when we are losing money and may have to cut our own people out of a job. You heard what he said about consultants, pet peeve, remember?"

"Jack, you know this is not the same. Did you explain it to him?"

"I did the best I could, Barry."

"What if I talked to him about it, Jack?"

"No, I don't think that would be a good idea. He has a lot going on and he prefers that people follow the chain of command."

"I don't know what to say." I had no idea where to turn now.

"I have a better idea." Jack smiled.

"What?"

"We think you should teach it. You did a good job with the Crosby training and ISO and SPC; you would do a great job."

I could not believe my ears. "I'm not qualified to do this, Jack. The trainers are experts in this stuff. I just heard about it a week ago."

"You told me it was not complex and besides, it needs to be customized for our business anyway."

"I said the actual concepts were not complex, but making a change this big in the way we look at the business, and the statistics and training, are over my head. After I have been through the whole training curriculum a couple times maybe, but now, not a chance. We only have one shot at this and if we blow it, we don't get a second chance."

"It's not me, Barry. Just give it your best shot. I have confidence in you. You can make it work."

"Right, Jack, talk to you later."

I was depressed. I bet he never even mentioned Six Sigma to Bob. How could he think I could do this on my own? He did not understand it even after I had spent hours explaining it to him. I needed to talk to Russ, but not now. I had to think this thing out. I had better get the old resume up-to-date I thought.

━ ━

I finally decided to call Russ that afternoon. The conversation with Jack was just preying on my mind. I had to talk to someone who would understand. I could not wait any longer.

"Hi, may I speak to Russ Peterson?"

"Russ is on the phone right now, would you like to hold or leave a message?"

"I'll hold."

Several minutes later, "Hello, Barry."

"Huh, oh, hi, Russ." I switched to the handset.

"What's new?" Russ sounded upbeat.

"Bad news," I said sadly.

"How is that?"

"I had Jack sold on the idea of Six Sigma, but he couldn't get his new boss convinced to spend the money."

"That's too bad."

"You haven't heard the funniest part. Jack wants me to teach Six Sigma." I waited for Russ's response.

"Wish I could say I never heard that one Barry, but I have. Unfortunately, it takes a special person with a lot of years of experience using Six Sigma to teach it effectively. Another negative is that people know you too well there. You need credibility because you are going to need people to have faith that this works and do things they might not initially agree with. Once they see that it works, then you could teach them, but not now."

"I was not even entertaining the idea, really. I just don't know what to do. Should I go over Jack's head and talk to Bob directly?"

"What would Jack say about that?"

"He already told me no, and I need his approval anyway."

"Well, Barry, Six Sigma has to be supported from the top. You can get by without the bottom of the organization on board at first because you can win them over. You will be making their lives easier. But the guy at the top, you need him to support you over the hump period."

"What's the hump period, Russ?"

"Whenever an organization does something as self-critical as Six Sigma, it creates a lot of stress."

"But we won't be trying to blame people, will we?" I didn't understand.

"It doesn't matter. People have a lot of pride and ego tied up in their jobs. When you suggest there is a better way to do something, and someone has done that job for 25 years, they feel stress that you are blaming them for doing it wrong or not finding a better way and somehow they will be found at fault."

"This company does point fingers a lot. You think people will be afraid of Six Sigma, Russ?"

"You have a union right?"

"Yes."

"Don't unions think everything the company does is a way to reduce the workforce?"

"You do have a point there."

"This is no different. You need to have people understand the rules are changing. You need their help. One thing we have not talked about yet is an *event*."

"What does that mean, an event?" I asked.

"What will happen if you announce you are implementing Six Sigma? What will people think?"

I wasn't sure where Russ was taking this. "I guess they probably think this is just another quality program. Flavor of the month?"

"Exactly, Barry. If you can, you need a defining event that makes people take notice."

"Like what, Russ?"

"When I was at Exponex, when we started Six Sigma we took all our rejects and put them out front where people could see us scrap them."

"Why?"

"Because we quit reworking bad electronics. We had too many complaints. So we made a decision to scrap all bad units. People knew if we made bad units, there was no second chance."

"Wow. Did it work?"

"Absolutely. It was the talk of the plant. Everyone knew the rules had changed."

"I can't see us piling our products out front, Russ." I shook my head.

"No. That is not your defining event. You have to figure it out. Believe me, you will know it when you find it."

"Well if I don't get upper management approval, what can I do?" I was really dejected.

"Barry, there is nothing you can do but keep selling Six Sigma to your people. Don't be obnoxious, just keep selling."

"OK, Russ. Wish me luck."

11

Step Up to the Plate

The next few months were terrible. I saw so many possibilities to apply Six Sigma to our situation. And I let Jack know about it every chance I could get. I wasn't pushy, but it got to the point where he would say "And I know, Barry, if we were doing Six Sigma, this would not be happening." And I would just smile.

On Monday morning I checked my messages and was surprised to find I already had one at 7:00 a.m. I hit the play button on the machine.

"Hi, Barry. This is Jack. I need to see you today at 9:00 a.m. downtown. If there is a problem with this, please give Tamara a call. Thanks."

I wondered what was up, but I doubted it was good news. I got ready to head downtown.

"Hi, Tamara," I said as I walked down the hall. "I had a message to see Jack at 9:00 this morning."

"Come on in, Barry," said Jack as he heard me from his office.

As soon as I entered Jack's office I saw that Bob was sitting there too. He got up and patted me on the shoulder as I walked in.

Bob said, "Sorry I couldn't make that meeting with you a few months ago, but I have been really busy trying to get a feel for this business."

"No problem, Mr. Jones," I said as I sat in the chair he offered me at the table in the corner.

"Call me Bob." He sat in the chair opposite mine at the round table.

I had to admit the guy had a way of making you feel at ease. He reminded me of Russ the way he did that. I wondered where you learned how to do that. He just made you feel good somehow.

"What Jack and I asked you down for was for me to learn more about this Six Sigma idea you have." He smiled at me.

I was speechless. I looked at Jack and he smiled at me.

I said, "Uh, well, uh, I really have a lot to learn about it myself but I am sure we need it."

"Well, it sounds like something we need to seriously consider," Bob replied.

Jack spoke up. "Well, Barry, when Bob asked me about our plans to improve our operations recently, I realized we needed something to change. And then I realized I did not have the answer. But you were so convinced you did have the answer, I wanted Bob to hear about Six Sigma from you."

Bob said, "I see you have been on the management team here for only a short time, Barry. This plant is especially important to our division because of the volume you produce."

"I am aware of that, Bob."

Bob continued, "I am going to be perfectly honest with you, Barry. We cannot continue to operate this plant losing money. It has to be profitable."

"I certainly understand that. That is the requirement of any business," I said confidently.

"Some people don't see it that way. Our division is making money and the corporation is profitable, but we won't stay in business if we lose money. We just can't. Some of our other plants are beginning to struggle too."

"You don't have to convince me. I agree."

"OK. So tell me about Six Sigma, Barry."

I told Bob all about Six Sigma. After we had finished, I looked down at my watch and I realized we had been talking for nearly two hours.

"I didn't mean to take up your whole morning, Bob."

Bob smiled and said, "That's OK, Barry. I like what I hear, but I would like to learn more. It sounds good. For the record, I am against consultants doing work we can do ourselves. But this sounds more like an investment in our future. I like that."

"Exactly!" I replied. Boy, it was nice to have someone grasp the concepts so quickly.

Bob said, "I sure wish something like this was around when I was in the trenches. Let's get these Six Sigma experts down here and see what the rest of our people think about it. You mentioned that they did some type of executive training."

"Yes, they have executive training for top management."

"Who do you want to be there, Barry?" said Bob.

"Well, you of course and Jack. I would like for Henry to be there for finance, Jimmy for sales, Mark for R&D, Steve from manufacturing, and Howard from engineering."

"How about someone from HR, Barry?" said Jack.

"Great idea. We'll get Joe from HR also. Let's see, that's nine including me. I'll ask Dave if he would recommend anyone else. Any problem if I ask Russ Peterson to come down?"

"No, I would love to meet him after what you have told me."

"Great, well I will let you know when so we can coordinate our schedules."

"Sounds good. Let me know if I can help," Bob said as we walked out into the hall.

"Bye, Tamara," I said as I walked down the hall smiling.

━ ━

I was more optimistic than I had been at any time during my career at HPZ. It was great to work for someone who had a sense of what made a manufacturing plant tick. I had discussed all of my ideas with Bob and the best part of all is that he agreed this nonsense about our process being an art was exactly that—nonsense. He had worked at some plants in his career that talked that same language until they got a handle on things. They had used some techniques similar to Six Sigma, but he admitted it appeared that Six Sigma was a much more complete package than anything he had seen before.

12

The Plan

I called Russ first thing the next morning to give him the good news, but he was out for the morning and I asked his secretary to have him call me as soon as he got in. Dave was always traveling so I knew he would have to call me back. I left a message on his cell phone at the same time.

I continued to read about Six Sigma and I found out that the Internet was a great source of information. From my Internet searches, I found dozens of Six Sigma companies offering training.

The phone on my desk was ringing when I got in after lunch and it was Dave calling me back.

"Hi, Dave," I replied.

"I got your message, Barry, and that week seems fine for me. I'll be bringing one of our partners, Roman Simpson, with me to help with the executive training class. It will take two days to complete."

"Great Dave, if we can do it Tuesday and Wednesday that week, that would be perfect."

"OK, Barry, plan on starting at 8:00 and ending at 4:00."

"You are the expert, Dave. I'll get it set up. Can you join Jack, Bob, and myself for dinner Monday night around 8:00? I'm going to ask Russ to go also."

"Sure. I would love to, Barry. How about Roman? Is he invited?"

"Absolutely, I can't wait to meet him," I said.

"OK, Barry, see you Monday night. Bye."

"Bye, Dave." I hung up the phone. I was getting more excited every day.

— ◄ ►—

I had gotten e-mails back from all of the people I had invited to executive training except Henry. I decided to give Henry a call to get things nailed down.

I called his extension, and he answered his phone, a rare occurrence.

"Hi, Henry, its Barry."

"Hi, Barry, I know what you want and I'm sorry I haven't got back with you." Henry was head of finance and information technology.

"I wanted to make sure you were going to make it to the Six Sigma training on Tuesday and Wednesday."

"Well, I have a conflict." He sounded unsure.

"We really need you there. Finance is a big part of Six Sigma. We need your people to help find the best projects and calculate savings and such."

"I really need to meet with the auditors those two days, Barry. Can you get me in another training class?"

"It's not really that kind of training, Henry, and there won't be another class like this one. We need you to be part of the team that decides to do this right or decides not to do it at all. You really have to be there to hear what it's all about." I was pleading.

"I just can't spare the time, Barry. Do you know what all I have going on?" He was starting to sound agitated.

"We are all busy, Henry."

"Tell you what. Whatever the others decide is fine with me. If it comes down to a vote, you vote for me. This stuff doesn't sound like it involves finance anyway."

"It doesn't work that way, Henry. We need you there and finance *is* an integral part of the process."

"Look, if Jack or Bob says I gotta go, I will be there. Otherwise, I have more important things to do."

Great, I thought to myself. My first test.

I left a message for Bob telling him Henry had more important things to do than attend the executive training. I got a very short phone message from Bob the next day. It simply said, "Henry will be there."

13

Executive Training Begins

I had reserved the conference room and I came in a little early to arrange the tables appropriately. The phone in the back of the room rang and the receptionist informed me that I had visitors in the lobby. I hurried down to meet them.

They were examining our display cabinets in the lobby. We had a nice presentation there that included samples of our products and our quality certificate and awards from over the years. I thought about how good our company looked from the outside. As quality manager, it was my job to host customers when they came to check us out. I would show them our certificates and equipment and all of the procedures we had in place and our graphs hanging on the wall. I could put on quite a dog and pony show, and everyone played their parts well. Once you started looking deeper, however, we had so many fundamental problems. We even let our own act convince us that everything was all right. We should have seen this downturn in profitability coming a long time ago and started preparing for it.

"Good morning, gentlemen."

"Good morning, Barry," said Dave.

"If you will follow me upstairs, I'll show you where we'll be having the training sessions," I said.

The group followed me up the stairs and into the conference room.

⟶ ⟶

Roman and Dave started setting up their equipment. They had the training material in a PowerPoint presentation and copies in binders for all of the participants. They had a computer projector, and they started hooking up all the wires to get the show up and running.

"Do you need anything?" I asked.

"We try to bring everything we need, makes it easier. Thanks for asking though. We may need something later on," said Dave.

"OK, let me know if you do." I got out of their way as they connected the wires and plugged in the equipment.

While the Six Sigma guys were getting ready, the participants started showing up. I had put the binders on the tables with a pad and pencil for each person. The first person to show was Mark, our R&D director.

"Good morning, Barry." Mark had a PhD in chemistry. He was a bright guy. He had been with HPZ for nearly 25 years. Mark was responsible for new product development too.

"Hi, Mark, welcome." I motioned for him to take a seat anywhere.

"I hear you are going to teach us how to solve all the mysteries of making our products today," he said sarcastically.

"Not me, but these folks are going to show us how to help ourselves." I introduced the guests.

One problem with our product development was that we never developed anything really new. To be honest, we just copied what other companies were already doing. Sometimes our copycat products did not perform as well as the ones we copied.

Henry, Jimmy, and Steve came in next, followed by Joe. Henry glared at me as he took a seat. I guess he had not gotten over me going over his head to get him there.

Steve and Joe came up and said hello and got a cup of coffee. Joe was head of human resources and a great guy. He handled all of the personnel and union matters as well as some training efforts. Steve was an older guy; he ran our manufacturing group. He was fairly new to our plant and hired from the outside a few years ago.

We were still waiting on Howard, Jack, and Bob to get started. They came in a few minutes later and sat down in the second row. Bob gave me thumbs up.

"Ready?" I asked Dave.

"When you are. Everyone here?"

"Looks like it."

Dave started out by talking about the tools of Six Sigma and how computers made them easier to use.

"Dave, what are these tools and what do computers have to do with Six Sigma?" asked Henry. Henry was also responsible for computer resources in the plant as well as finance.

"Well, many of the tools are statistics-based, Henry. We will study them in more detail later. Statistics are an integral part of Six Sigma. Statistics allow us to make better decisions from data we collect, and also have more confidence in our decisions. The computers make using statistics easier. What used to be painstaking is much easier now."

"What type of computers and software are needed?" Henry continued.

"Your basic laptop and a statistics software package. You can use any statistics package, but our training materials are designed around Minitab so it makes it easier on our trainers really. Do you have a statistics package you are currently using?"

Henry turned and looked at me and I shook my head no.

Henry jotted down the information. "Are you familiar with our ERP software system, and is this statistics software compatible with the information we are getting from it?"

"I know a little about ERP systems, Henry. The software we use does not communicate directly with your software, but you can download data from your system and use the statistics software to analyze it."

"Well our software system is designed to help us make these decisions already Dave, so I don't know if we need this Six Sigma stuff at all." Henry was really proud of our new computer system.

Russ started smiling and said, "Henry, I've seen a lot of computer systems advertised to lead you to believe they will run your company for you. Do you know what is missing from these computer systems?"

"No, what?" Henry said.

"First, you don't know if the data is valid because the inputs are coming from measurement systems that have not been validated. Second, you may not even be collecting the right kind of information or even know what to be collecting. But most of all, once you have all this data, you don't even know how to use it. Data is only useful if you know what variables control your process. You have to identify the critical control points responsible for producing the output you desire and collect data on these inputs in a correct manner."

"Are you saying our ERP system is worthless?" Henry said sounding disturbed.

"Not at all," Russ continued. "Data is always needed and having the information readily available in real time is a wonderful tool. But only something that maximizes your human resource to discover new opportunities will create the improvements you are looking for."

"Thanks," said Henry obviously not satisfied.

"Can you tell me why you are here, Russ?" asked Steve.

"Good question, Steve. I have been asked that by a few people already. You supply our company with pigment, and I need good suppliers. Six Sigma will make you a better supplier with lower costs. Then you can pass that lower cost down to the consumer, me, who can then become more competitive."

Steve replied, "Thanks."

I was amazed that Steve agreed to Russ's comments. He usually had to have the last say in everything.

Bob was sitting in the back row and saying very little. I watched his reaction to all the questions. He listened intently. I had never met anyone who could listen more attentively than he did.

Dave asked, "Who can tell me what CTQ stands for?" No one answered.

"Critical to quality." He let it sink in for a minute. "Do you know what your customers want and need from your company?"

Jimmy answered. "Sure. They want quality products on time every time." Jimmy was king of the buzzwords at HPZ.

"But do you really know specifically what each customer needs?" asked Dave prodding.

We all looked at each other. Jimmy said, "Well probably not to every detail."

"Should you? Is anything else more important?" Dave asked.

"Probably not." Jimmy replied.

Dave continued, "A simplistic way to look at it is, you are all here to serve the customer. Almost everything you do can impact the customer in some way or form even if it is only increasing the cost of the product they buy. If it does not help the customer, you probably should question whether you need to do it. You need to define how those things you do are critical to the customer."

Howard was head of our engineering department, and he reported to Steve. He asked, "It appears that most of the people going down the Six Sigma path are huge corporations. We are a small company compared to these companies. How does that affect us?"

Dave said, "I will let Roman answer that one, Howard."

"Well, Howard, you bring up a good point," Roman replied. "You are smaller than a Motorola for sure, but you perform all of the same elements in your plant as Motorola does. You develop new products, manufacture for customers, sell and ship on time, spend capital money to improve, maintain equipment, issue invoices, and so on. The scale of your Six Sigma deployment may be smaller, but it is really the same. I have worked with many small clients, some much smaller than this plant. Everything still applies. I think that will become more apparent as we continue the training."

"OK." Howard seemed satisfied with the answer for now.

Roman then described the roles played by each element in the organization, the executives, the champions, the Blackbelts and the Greenbelts.

Joe asked, "Now what is the difference between a Blackbelt and a Greenbelt again?"

Roman replied, "The major difference between the two is that Blackbelts get a full training package and work full-time on projects anywhere in the organization. Greenbelts receive less training and can be anyone in the organization from managers to production workers but work part-time on problems in their own work area. A plant this size might have 20 Blackbelts but 500 Greenbelts."

Joe added, "Do we train Blackbelts and Greenbelts together?"

"No," Roman answered. "The level of training is too different. The Blackbelts are actually used to train the Greenbelts in most companies. So Greenbelts come after initial Blackbelt training."

"What about the champions, Roman? Do they do projects?" Henry asked.

"Good question, Henry. The champions don't do projects, but they are a vital part of the support structure for the projects. Champions are typically the managers and leaders in the company and they make sure the Blackbelts and Greenbelts have everything they need to make the project successful. They are kind of like the business owners and the Blackbelts and Greenbelts are like the people they hire to get things done."

Roman continued, "There is one group in your company who is best prepared to make Six Sigma fail. Any idea who that might be?"

"Make it fail?" Jack asked. "Can Six Sigma fail?"

"Yes, it can fail to be what you want and need it to be," Roman said.

"Probably us," I said.

"Absolutely correct," said Roman. "The people in this room control the resources that make or break Six Sigma."

"How can you say that about us? You don't know us or this business," said Mark. He had a thin skin.

"This business is not as different as you think it is, Mark."

"Maybe Six Sigma just does not fit our business. Maybe it will not work here," said Henry.

Roman replied, "This business is run by people, right? Then Six Sigma fits. Six Sigma develops your human resource and that is the common element in any business. I like to say we turn your human resources into resourceful humans."

"Hey I like that resourceful humans thing," Joe said. "I agree with Roman, we need to do a better job training our people. We have good people and we still can't get things done. I think this will help. I like what I am hearing."

"I think we all know there are plenty of things to improve, but making our products is just so complex," said Mark. Mark was one of those 'making pigment is an art, not a science' disciples.

Bob voiced his first comments. "My answer to that, Mark, is, we are not profitable at this plant as we currently operate. Our markets indicate we cannot expect prices to escalate. If we can't improve, we will have to let someone else give it a try. I won't operate an unprofitable plant. So the question I see before us is whether we use Six Sigma or we use something else. Because we are going to do something. Anyone here know of something better?" Bob was dead serious.

No one said a word. You could hear a pin drop, on the carpet even.

"I am just worried that we won't have anyone to work on other things if everyone is doing this type of work," said Steve.

"What do you mean this type of work?" said Roman.

"You know, Six Sigma work."

"Steve, there is nothing different about Six Sigma work except that it is more efficient. I personally would want all my people working in this manner whether they are in production, engineering, or finance," Roman replied.

"I just need to know more about it."

"That is why we are here to help, Steve."

Dave spoke up, "Let's talk a little about the role of the Blackbelt during the training phase and after the training phase. That might make things a little clearer. As we said, the Blackbelts are the ones who will use the tools, but the champions will direct them to the appropriate projects. You and your managers are typically the champions of the process. You utilize the asset, the Blackbelts, and remove roadblocks from their path. You free them up to do what they do best, solve problems."

Dave continued, "The Blackbelt will undergo four weeks of training, but there will be three weeks between each of the training weeks to work on their training project. You will help select that training project. Later we will use some of the tools we will teach the Blackbelts so you will get some hands-on experience. We also provide Master Blackbelts to assist your Blackbelts during those three-week work periods. The training is approximately a five-month commitment, and we find that the savings from the training projects alone will pay for the training. After the training phase, a Blackbelt can handle four to six projects a year that may increase in difficulty as they gain experience."

Jimmy raised his hand and said, "How many of these Blackbelts do we need?"

Roman answered by saying, "You can have as many Blackbelts as you care to support is the answer. One caution though, Blackbelts require resources like team members and production time to run experiments and lab time for samples. Be careful you don't try too much at one time and overload your support systems. This is why most companies train their Blackbelts in waves."

"What do you mean waves?" said Joe.

"Waves are simply classes. Between 10 and 30 is a good class size. You would also want to spread the projects out over the different areas of the plant."

Bob commented, "So basically you are saying that we should start with a class of about 10 people in a wave and it takes about five months to get them trained. They work on individual projects during the training. Do they pass the projects on to the next class when they finish training?"

Dave smiled. "No one passes on a project. We do not certify a person as a Blackbelt unless they can show they have met their goal and solved the problem they were assigned."

"Really? Isn't that a lot of pressure to put on people?" asked Steve.

"It works. People want the certification and they want the recognition that comes with it, so they work hard. We have had people tell us it is the most work they have ever done, the most stress they have ever been under, and they loved every minute of it."

About that time lunch was brought in and we broke to eat. Bob cornered me away from the others. "Barry, I really like what I am hearing today."

"Me too, Bob, me too."

14

Executive Training: Define and Measure

During lunch I listened to the dialogue between our executives. It seemed that the message that Russ, Roman, and Dave were giving us was starting to sink in. Our representitive from HR, Joe, was already sold on the idea. He saw it as a way to empower the shop floor, which is something he had been trying to do for years. He especially liked that we would be training our own people to continue the training once the consultants were finished. He knew that all too often, once the consultants left, everything stopped. If we trained our own people it could continue as long as we wanted it too.

I listened as Steve and Howard were talking about who would make good Blackbelt candidates from their workforce. They ran manufacturing and had several people they wanted to move up in the organization. Six Sigma was a great grooming ground and a better proving ground.

Mark was still unconvinced, as he was talking to Henry and Dave. Mark didn't see how it fit with R&D. Dave explained how companies used Six Sigma to design quality into products before they started producing them. It was called DFSS, or design for Six Sigma. Mark just could not seem to shake off the idea that we were different. I had to work on him some more. A company that could not develop innovative products would ultimately lose out to those that could no matter how low-cost they were.

Henry did not seem to dislike Six Sigma. He just could not see that finance had to be involved. I told him I saw Six Sigma as a great tool to help decide how your money would best be spent. Roman told Henry that many companies do a special training class called "transactional quality" just for finance and other processes that involved transactions other than manufacturing. He explained that the cost of money was huge in a business like ours. We had huge sums tied up in raw materials, inventory, and goods in progress and we got no return from that money.

Jimmy, our sales guy, was starting to get excited. He told Jack he was counting on the new sales and new products. If you were a customer and wanted a long-term supply partner, who would be better than a company using Six Sigma, he said.

Bob listened more than he talked. Since he was new, this was a good way for him to learn what his executives believed. I felt like he had already decided to try Six Sigma at our plant.

After lunch was over, Dave took the floor.

"OK, any questions about what we covered before lunch? Good, then I want to cover what we call the typical road map for Six Sigma projects. We believe Six Sigma is a journey because every stop along the way is critical to reaching the destination. Sometimes we call it a journey from art to science."

Dave continued, "As I said, we call this set way of doing things our road map and it revolves around the five modules, which are *define*, *measure*, *analyze*, *improve* and *control*. But first, we need a team to help us. Who in your operation knows what really goes on in the plant?" Dave looked for someone to answer.

"That would be my people probably," said Mark. "They have the most education and experience."

"Really? Anyone disagree with Mark?"

I raised my hand and said, "The operators or whoever is doing the job know more than anyone."

"That is exactly right, Barry," Dave said.

"I disagree," said Mark. "Our operators don't even understand the chemistry of the process. How can they know more?"

Dave replied, "Well Mark, while operators may not know the chemistry, I bet they know what actually happens in their workplace. I bet they can tell you a good place to start working on fixing a problem. They may not be able to draw a flow sheet or balance a chemical equation, but they have a better understanding of what really goes on than your people may. What happens on the midnight shift on Sunday night? These things are the clues to what is causing your process to change unexpectedly."

"I really doubt that," said Mark.

Dave continued, "Trust me on this one, Mark. You need everyone on the team, especially the workers. You also need research and maintenance and labs and finance. The rule is to get everyone you can who knows anything about the problem at hand. This is the basis for your team."

Joe replied, "Mark, we need our hourly people to feel like they are a part of the team. If they are a part of the solution they will work to make it happen."

Mark was not budging on this one. He just looked away.

"OK," Dave said. "The team has to develop what we call the process map, which is used to document the existing process. We go into a lot of detail on process mapping in Blackbelt training because this is the basis for the rest of the project. It is very important to capture everything you know about the process on paper."

"What do you mean by everything, Dave?" said Jack.

"As an example, you may have a process where the operator may have noticed that things don't work the same on hot days versus cold days. So temperature becomes an X variable you need to study. Your engineers would not know this since it was not listed as a specification for the step. So temperature is included on your process map."

Mark remarked, "I still think making pigment is an art and there are some things we will never understand. This Six Sigma stuff may help some, but I wouldn't count on it solving 35-year-old problems."

I looked at Dave and threw up my hands.

"Its OK to be skeptical, Mark. All we ask is you have an open mind. OK?"

"My mind is always open," said Mark.

"OK, where were we? Process map. This is where all the possible variables are captured. Some will have no impact, but some will be very important. So how many do you think will be important?"

Nobody answered; we just looked around at each other.

Dave said, "I would estimate 20 percent of them would be important."

"Why 20 percent, Dave?" asked Jimmy.

"Ever heard of the Pareto principle?"

"Sure," said Steve. "Better known as the 80:20 rule."

"So the answer is, we really just want to identify the critical 20 percent variables and work on those first. That 20 percent will be responsible for 80 percent of our problem. See how we are starting to define the process? That's the first step in our DMAIC roadmap."

Howard said, "Yes I can see that, also it makes it a lot easier. We ignore the little stuff so we can focus on the big hitters."

"Exactly," Dave said. "We then rank the variables with something called a PFMEA or a process failure mode and effects analysis. It is basically controlled brainstorming. You rate every variable for potential of failure, ability to detect, and magnitude of effect. It is quite systematic. After the PFMEA, you will be able to prioritize the variables from the process map. This is how we start to identify our 20 percent."

Howard said, "Sounds like a lot of time involved with the PFMEA. Is it really necessary?"

Dave answered, "Would it take less time to choose the wrong variable to work on, perform experiments on these wrong variables, and then realize you had to start over?"

"I suppose not," Howard said sheepishly.

Dave continued, "OK, next we come to the one thing a lot of companies miss that causes a lot of problems, measurement error. Do you perform any measurements here?"

"Boy do we," I exclaimed. "Sometimes I think we measure too much."

"Well, how do you know these measurements are accurate?" Dave stood back and folded his hands behind his back.

"Well, we have a general idea, we have done some studies," I answered.

Mark replied, "Oh yes, John Adams works for me and he has done some repeats on most of the tests at some time or another."

Dave asked, "Does this guy John run all of your tests for you?"

Mark answered, "No, no, he is in charge of the research lab. We have technicians in the process who run all the plant samples and final products. John does not actually run the tests for the plant."

Dave smiled a little and said, "How do you know the technicians get the same numbers as John, and who knows if John is actually right." I got the feeling he had seen this before.

"Well, John has been here for 30 years and has run every test we have," Mark replied with utmost confidence.

"OK, so how does John run these repeats?"

"He takes a sample and runs it ten times and compares the numbers. He gets pretty much the same answer every time so the tests have to be good. And he uses statistics to analyze it too," Mark said proudly.

Dave said, "A little word of advice; people usually get the same answer if they know what the answer is supposed to be." Dave winked at me. "Want to know the right way to find out if your tests are any good?"

I said, "Yes," quite loudly.

"A good gage R&R study, which stands for repeatability and reproducibility, has several requirements. It needs to be blind so participants don't know the answer, and performed by the people who normally run the test, all of them. You might have one person who does not run it right and that person could be the one that analyzes that important sample you make a decision based on. You want to have samples across the range of the test. The test may be good at the low end of the range but not the high end. You must run enough repeats over a long enough time period to make sure you capture day-to-day variation. And it needs to be random. Who can tell me why randomization is important?"

No one answered.

"Randomization is very important for a lot of reasons, but mostly so you don't draw false conclusions. Let's say you let lab person A run all of their samples on Monday and lab person B runs all of theirs on Friday, instead of half for each person both days. You notice lab person B gets higher values. You call them in and say, 'you have a problem, lab person B, your results are higher than A.' Anyone see a problem here?"

"I do," said Howard. "The real problem may be that the instruments were reading higher on Friday, or the humidity in the lab was higher, and had nothing to do with lab person B."

"Exactly. Randomization would prevent this false assumption."

"Wow, we have a lot to work to do. We have never done anything like that here before," said Jimmy.

"Why is the measurement stage at the beginning of the road map?" Dave asked.

Jack said, "I would expect that garbage in is garbage out right?"

"Yes. How can you run experiments in the improve phase if your tests are not accurate? You won't be able to tell anything. Believe me when I tell you it is a big problem everywhere. The fact that you have been running a test for 35 years gives you no proof the test is good."

Mark was shaking his head 'no' the whole time Dave was talking.

Dave said, "OK, let's review for a minute. What is the road map for our Six Sigma process?"

Steve said, "DMAIC which stands for define, measure, analyze, improve, and control."

"And what major tools do we use in the define phase Steve?"

"Well, let's see. First we form our team so we have the people we need to be able to define the process we are working on. And I guess the main tools are the process map and the PFMEA."

Dave continued, "Good job. Yes, the team participates in everything. The process map defines the steps in the process and the inputs and outputs. The PFMEA then characterizes these variables and allows us to sort them based on importance to our problem. You are doing so well Steve, now tell us about the measure phase."

"I suppose the measurement process is what we are examining in the measure phase. So the gage R&R would be the main tool there." Steve looked at Dave for approval.

Dave said proudly, "I think we have the beginnings of a good Blackbelt here folks. The gage R&R is indeed our primary tool for the measurement phase. I repeat: we must have good measurements if we want to be successful with the analyze, improve, and control phases."

Roman added, "There are many other things we also teach, like capability assessment, Pareto analysis, and defects analysis, but this covers the major parts of the define and measurement phases. Any questions?"

"How about a break, Dave? These chairs are getting pretty hard," said Jack.

"Good idea, Jack. Let's take a 20-minute break and we will start back up at 2:00 p.m. talking about the analyze phase."

I walked over to Bob and shook my head. "I'm worried about our measurements, Bob. After what Dave said, I have no confidence at all in them. Half the time out in production, the operators don't believe the lab results. If our tests are not right, it's like flying blind."

"No, it's worse than that, Barry. No test at all is flying blind. Wrong test results are much worse. Think about it."

I thought about it. We could be making the process worse by changing things based on bad test results. It would be like flying a plane and your instruments said you were climbing above your target altitude when you were really descending. If you made an adjustment you would descend even more. If you were off by enough, you would crash into the ground. That is when I realized how important our test results were: they were our guidance system for the plant.

15

Executive Training: Analyze

"**R**oman is going to talk about the analyze phase. We will not go deeply into it because it gets pretty heavy into statistics," Dave said.

"Oh great," said Henry. "I knew we would get hit with statistics sooner or later. My head hurts already."

"It won't be that bad, Henry. Remember that your Blackbelts will get 40 hours of training plus three weeks of support doing project work on this phase alone. Don't expect us to be able to teach you the same thing in a couple of hours. We just want you to get a feel for the methodology. You don't have to master these tools, that is why you have the Blackbelts."

"That's a relief," said Henry, but we all felt that way.

Roman stood up front and asked, "OK, I have a question for you. Who here has had a class in statistics before?"

Most everyone in the room raised their hand.

"OK, well I guess I can skip this phase since everyone knows how to use statistics to analyze data and make confident decisions."

Bob replied, "I wouldn't go that far."

"Why is that, Bob?"

"Well, Roman, I took a class in college and I could not wait to get out of there. I remember very little about it except the general stuff everyone knows like mean and median and mode."

Roman asked the group, "Anyone feel confident using statistics?"

No one raised their hand.

Henry replied, "No one really understands the stuff."

Roman answered, "The reason is that statistics are generally taught without association with real events. When they are applied to things that happen in the "real world," they start to make sense. That is why Blackbelts are able to apply statistics successfully after Six Sigma."

I thought back to the test Bill ran in 1985. We thought the quality was poorer. We didn't know that for sure, we just guessed. It would have been nice to have something to tell us we were making the best decision.

Roman continued, "We teach people how to collect data. How to calculate the appropriate sample size. Then use statistical tools like t-tests, f-tests, analysis of variance, and many others. We look for trends using correlation and regression analysis. We calculate confidence intervals."

Mark whined, "All I know is that with statistics you can prove anything. A pigment plant does not respond like a widget plant. This is a chemical plant we are running here. We don't make widgets."

Roman calmly replied, "Well Mark, it does not matter if it is a chemical plant or a widget plant or a service industry or a medical business, there are ways to make better decisions using statistics. As far as proving *anything* with statistics, remember when Dave said this was a rigid methodology? Statistics is a science and there are right ways and wrong ways to apply the science. We teach Blackbelts the right way."

Russ added, "In organizations that use Six Sigma, it is never the researcher's reputation that's on the line for decision making. If we had a common problem-solving methodology, we would all arrive at the same decision if we looked at the same set of data. We would all analyze the data in the same manner and reach the same conclusions. If the decision is wrong, and it will be sometimes, it is not the person who is at fault. That is just the way the cards were dealt. Nothing has 100 percent confidence. The main thing is we all know we did the best we could and we keep on working until we get it right."

I just sat there thinking about all the bad feelings and gossip and rumors that existed in our plant. A lot of it would not exist if we had something to help us make decisions. We were constantly blaming each other for our problems.

Russ added, "You just learned one of the side benefits of Six Sigma: people communicate better and get along better when they have a set way to do something. No one gets offended over your opinion of something because we don't make decisions based on opinion any longer."

Roman said, "The analyze phase is really important. Sometimes if there is enough existing data about the process, the Blackbelt can figure out which of the X variables are the right ones to improve just by analyzing the data, but not typically."

I looked around and saw puzzled looks on people's faces. "You might want to go into a little more detail on this Roman," I replied.

"Sure, Barry. The problem is we nearly always have a lot more variables identified during our define and measurement phases than we could ever hope to work on efficiently. We need a way to pull out the critical few variables from the trivial many variables. Remember the 80:20 rule."

Dave added, "It is a real problem when you get to the improve phase, where experiments are needed to determine what we can control to make the process better. Anyone ever try to run an experiment with a dozen variables? Almost impossible to get meaningful information if we have that many variables. Not to mention the cost and time involved. It is crucial to whittle the number of variables down as low as possible, and still be as sure as we can that we have those critical 20 percent included."

Roman continued, "Dave is exactly right. The best way to do this is using statistics. If random variation is responsible for the differences we see in our data, we can identify that. For example, let's assume the people in this room are a representative sample of the population of people on this site. And we want to determine if the average weight of people working in manufacturing is higher than the average weight of people not in manufacturing. We can do that with a t-test."

Roman asked everyone working in the plant to list their weight. He put the weights of people from manufacturing in one column on the flipchart and everyone else in a second column. He plugged the numbers into the computer program and generated a t-test statistic.

Roman continued as he pointed to the data on the screen. "What we are asking ourselves is if the variable of "where we work" has an influence on our weight. In reality, this variable can be anything. It might be if one raw material had different effect than another. Or if one piece of equipment produces different parts versus another. Or if one customer survey is more effective than another. Or if one method of repairing something lasts longer than another."

It was starting to make sense to people now.

Roman continued, "So you see, the t-test statistic takes the data and compares it using a distribution function allowing calculation of a probability that the two groups are really different. We look for a p-value of less than 0.05 if we want to say with 95 percent confidence that there is a difference in weight based upon where we work. In this case there is not since the p-value is 0.25."

Jimmy said, "I think I understand now. Since where we work does not show up as a significant variable for weight, we might want to rule it out as one of our critical variables."

"Exactly," said Roman.

"And that means we can now concentrate on our other variables such as diet?" asked Joe.

"Heh, you are getting the picture. Finding the critical variables is sometimes a process of elimination. If we know what is not causing the problem, we can concentrate on finding the real problem with our experimentation using a workable number of variables," said Dave.

Roman added, "The tools we teach in the analyze phase are useful for a lot more too, it's just too much to go into in such a short period of time. You will just have to trust us when we say that after the Blackbelts are trained they will be able to differentiate real differences from random variation. And determine how much of an effect a variable has on something of importance. And develop a formula for the relationship between variables. And so much more."

Dave said, "There is nothing magic about statistics, folks. It's just a way to be more confident in your decision making. Insurance companies use statistics all the time to decide who to insure and how much to charge and still make a profit. See any of the big insurance companies going out of business? OK, that's enough for today, and we will see you tomorrow to talk about the improve phase."

16

Executive Training: Improve

Russ had revealed another one of Six Sigma's side benefits to me over dinner the night before. He told me how he used to be constantly swamped by people asking for his opinion before they started their Six Sigma initiative at Exponex. No one seemed to want to make a decision without his approval.

Russ said some of the problem was his own reluctance to let people make their own decisions. But at the time, he did not have confidence in their decision-making abilities.

After Six Sigma, he said, it was very different. When he got a call from a manager about what to do, he just followed the Six Sigma road map. Did you check the measurements for accuracy? Have we performed a capability study on that process to see if it can perform at that level? Did you ask the customer if that is critical to quality for them? Have you identified the critical X variables? What did the hypothesis test tell you about the results of the experiment? When are you going to run the DOE?

After a while, the managers started calling him with the answers to their problems instead of the problems themselves. They knew what to do and how to do it. They knew what he was going to ask them. He had more confidence in their decision making, and the managers had more confidence in themselves.

He started leaving the office earlier. He quit getting calls on the weekends. He did not have fifty voice mails and a hundred e-mails to answer when he got back from a two-day business trip. He said it was great. He had time to focus on managing and growing the business, which was what he was really supposed to be doing.

I thought about how many meetings we had that wasted people's time while we tried to reach a consensus on evaluating data or making a decision. I remembered the meeting we had after the test in 1985. We had high-level people tied up for hours. That kept them away from real work. No wonder everyone at our plant was behind all the time. I also realized that we did it so others could share the blame if things did not work.

I met Russ, Roman, and Dave on the way to the conference room. While we were setting up the room, Jimmy came in and sat down.

Jimmy asked, "Will Six Sigma help us to get product out on time to customers, Barry?"

"Who are we late shipping now, Jimmy?"

"Who are we not late shipping?" Jimmy responded. "Our poor production rate last month caught up with us and we have to delay shipments to almost everyone."

Russ, Roman, and Dave listened as we talked. The other people started drifting in and appeared to be interested in our conversation as well.

"I was in the warehouse yesterday, Jimmy, we have lots of inventory. The warehouse is almost half full."

"It may be half full, but I don't have what the customers want. Here are the inventory list and current orders. You try and fill these orders with that inventory."

I went over and looked at the inventory list. "Well these two trucks can ship. Hytec Industries buys P-101 and we have two trucks in inventory."

Jimmy looked over my shoulder. "Hytec Industries requires material in the orange-band, cone-bottom super sacks. That material is in the red-band, flat-bottom sacks. They won't take it."

"OK, what about 3G Minerals here? They want P-115 and we have 200 tons in stock."

"Nope. 3G has to have low pH material and all that is too high for them."

I said, "Here's some low pH material, what's wrong with this?"

Jimmy looked at the sheet. "Uhh, oh. 3G will only take 4-way pallets so they can reuse them. This is on 2-way pallets and it's not shrink-wrapped."

I was really starting to get frustrated. "OK, how about this 300 tons of P-112SP. I know that's good stuff. Someone must want that."

"It's in 25-kg bags instead of 50-lb bags. Remember that order we had last year for Europe and we had production problems and missed the ship date. When we finally got the order made, the customer said forget it because they had already bought from the competition in Europe."

"You mean to tell me, Jimmy, we have 6000 tons of inventory and we can't sell any of it!"

"I didn't say I could not sell it. It's just not what the customer wants. We can rework it or I can sell it at a discount, but we don't *want* to spend any extra money or sell at discount since we are so far in the hole after last month."

I shook my head in disgust.

Russ spoke up, "Let me see if I can add anything here. You have product in the warehouse but it's in the wrong package or the wrong type or off in some quality parameter to meet the customer's requirement?"

Jimmy said, "Exactly."

"Do a lot of your customers want special packaging or special requirements, Jimmy?"

"More and more, Russ. We actually turn away a lot of business because we already have so many SKUs and we can't manage what we have. If production had their way we would make only one product in one package type."

"And Barry, it costs extra to rework it?" Russ asked.

I replied. "If I have to re-bag or reprocess, it certainly eliminates any profit we might make from it. We just are not set up to do that, and then you risk contamination from the extra handling and you always lose some in the process of reworking."

"So what typically happens to this type of material that stays in the warehouse, Jimmy?"

Jimmy said, "We usually hold on to it until we find someone to take it or we rework it if we get desperate for something to ship."

"OK. Dumb question, but why not just fill the orders for the customers as the orders come in instead of making for inventory?" asked Russ.

"Let me explain," I told Jimmy. " We would love to, but we take all of these special requirements from customers and we don't charge anything extra for it. We only make certain grades at a time. We have about 15 products and only 5 production lines so we have to campaign products. It costs a lot to change over and it's hard to do, so we try to make at least two weeks worth if we can. We try to predict what the customer's demands will be until the next run and inventory it. We pack it in the customer's requested package and, after we test it, *then* we find out something like the pH is wrong. So now we have it in the wrong package for people who will buy high pH and no product for the low-pH people. Add to this the fact that we have to test for a dozen different things and it just gets too complicated to keep up with it. I've asked sales to restrict all this special requirement stuff. We used to sell everything in 50-lb white bags and that's what everybody got. It was a lot simpler back then."

Russ sighed. "Well it's like this, Barry: if you don't give the customer what they want, they will go somewhere else and get it. It is really an advantage if you do something the competition doesn't do, like special packaging, even if it sells for the same price. Think about it as the customer: would you want to pay more for a bag that works better for you when the material has to come in a bag anyway?"

I said, "Well, I guess not, but it just complicates our lives so much. But you are right. Customers don't care how my life is complicated. That's my job to fix it and give them what they want." I looked over at Jimmy. Jimmy had a smug look on his face and I wanted to wipe it off.

Russ continued, "The next thing is, you are already in the make-to-order business, you just do not realize it and you aren't very good at it. The fact that you cannot control what is coming out of your plant and don't know what you have until it gets through inspection is what is causing all the problems for you. If you could dial in the product to meet what your customers wanted, would it be a problem to fill the orders, say, in 30 days, Jimmy?"

"30 days would be great. We typically take longer than that now. Almost all of our customers give us a 30-day lead time."

"Could you predict, based on order pattern, your requirements for three months for, say, 80 percent of your customers?"

"Let me see. Sure I think so. We don't sell that many new customers really and it's not like customers change their requirements very often. 80 percent is probably realistic."

Russ added, "Barry, you need to start working on defining the variables in your process that cause you the most problems in meeting the special requirements for the customers Jimmy gives you. Then Jimmy can give you a production plan for them several months in advance. Pack out what the customer needs in their special packaging by controlling those variables. Fill the order as close as possible to when the order has to be shipped. If you only make the product once in a while, try to find ways to cut the costs and reduce the time involved in changeovers so you don't need to inventory as much between runs."

It was Mark's turn to speak up, "Russ, you just don't seem to realize this is a pigment plant and not a widget plant. It takes a lot of time to change grades and we make a lot of intermediate product. Things that work in plants making widgets won't work here. They just won't. We cannot be in the special-order business."

Jimmy added, "Russ, I can't afford to get any farther behind in shipments. We have always tried to inventory at least two months worth of product so we have something to ship when it is ordered. I get calls every day asking about deliveries."

Russ smiled, "It is a different concept, but I promise you it is the better way. Any idea what the cost of inventorying several months of product is, Henry?"

Henry thought for a minute. "Let's see. We produce 20 million dollars worth of product a month so say 40 million dollars just in inventory. Add to that outside warehouse costs and movements. Carrying costs on the money would be a million at least."

Steve added, "Don't forget personnel and damage. We have to move the stuff around to find the right pigment to ship and we damage product with the forklifts. We need extra people to move it around. All of the repackaging costs and rework too, when it is in the wrong bags. We pay for that too. If we got the right stuff in the right bag, we wouldn't need to discount it. I bet all of that is worth several million if not more."

I added, "I would say it is easily 5 million a year."

Russ said, "So we are talking about some real money here, right?"

"Absolutely."

"Think about it. We made things a lot more complex than pigment to-order at Exponex, and you will find it is easier than trying to inventory a lot of different products. The way you inventory now, you still don't have the right things to ship. I promise you it will be less expensive and you will meet more orders on time. Jimmy, I would encourage your salespeople to not only accept special requirement orders from customers but also to go out and promote it. When you do something special that your competition does not do, it makes you harder to replace as a supplier. It is in your best interest to do something out of the ordinary. When the customer sends out bids for low pH pigment in 25-kg purple bags, you can do that quickly at no extra cost while the competition may not be set up to do it. Plus, if you do what I have suggested, you will make more money. The secret is that the customer does not have to pay for it, the savings come out of your waste."

I looked at Jimmy and the rest of the group. "I think I have someone's Blackbelt project."

Dave said, "You probably have several people's projects, Barry."

Dave and Roman went up to the front of the room.

Dave started by asking, "Who makes the best Blackbelt, the one who has worked in the problem area their entire career or someone who has never set foot there?"

Mark popped his head up and said, "The person who knows the area best of course. They already have an edge because they work there."

Roman answered, "Many times the person who is too close to the problem has a hard time listening to his team and thinks they know the answer before they get started. I like to use an experienced Blackbelt from outside the area because they don't rule anything out and listen better."

Mark huffed, "I don't buy that. You have to know something about something to be able to fix it."

Roman added, "That is what the team is for Mark."

Mark wasn't buying it. There did not seem to be much he agreed with concerning the Six Sigma philosophies.

Roman continued, "Who knows what DOE stands for?"

Henry said, "Department of Energy?"

We all laughed. "No, it stands for design of experiments, but good try."

Henry laughed, "Hey, I'm an accountant, not a scientist!"

"Well, DOE is the basis behind our improve phase. During this week of training we teach the Blackbelt how to identify and manipulate the X variables that are responsible for the Y variable we want to control. Has anyone had any experience with this before?"

Howard raised his hand. "I have a little bit. I tried some when I first came here five years ago on the reactors, but it didn't show us anything. After that, people said that DOE was a waste of time. Now I find out the reason is the measurement process probably wasn't good enough."

"Good, Howard. That's a great point to make. Well, the best way to learn about DOE is hands-on experience. So we are going to let you do your own DOE."

Dave had reached in a bag and pulled out two wooden contraptions that looked liked someone's science fair project.

"What in the world is that?" asked Jimmy.

Russ said, "That is called a Statapult. It is a mini-catapult that you can use to learn about DOE. Let me explain how it works."

Russ showed us how the catapult worked. It was pretty simple really. It used rubber bands to provide tension on an arm that you pulled back and then let go to launch a ball. There were several adjustable parts on the catapult. You could use one or two rubber bands to provide the tension. The tension on the rubber bands could also be adjusted with a pin that could be placed in one of four holes. The cup that held the ball could be placed in one of two holes. And the angle of the arm could be controlled by how far you pulled back the arm. Depending on the setup, the ball went only a few feet or nearly across the room.

Dave started explaining how the DOE process worked. "A DOE allows you to model a process and develop a mathematical formula that can predict how a process will react under different conditions. When we have a model, we can then calculate how changing the X variables will affect the output response, our Y variable."

There were a lot of puzzled faces.

Dave continued, "Let me see if I can explain it a little simpler for you. Our process today is the shooting of the balls with the catapult. We are concerned with the distance the ball travels. In your factory the process might be the yield of one of your catalysts or the color of the product. So what type of variable is the distance the ball travels or the color or the yield?"

Jack answered, "That would be the Y variable, of course, since it is the output of the process."

We all looked at Jack amazed. It appeared he was getting more of this than we thought he would.

"Absolutely 100 percent correct. So, the adjustments I showed you on the catapult—what would they be?"

Jack continued, "The X variables, since they control the distance the ball travels."

"Great, now if I want you to shoot the ball 10 feet, how would you set up the catapult?" Dave smiled.

We all looked at each other. No one really knew where to start.

Joe said, "I guess we would just try some set of conditions to see if it works. And keep trying until we found something that did."

Dave replied, "That's how a lot of people do it. What happens when you find a setup that shoots the ball 10 feet?"

Joe answered, "I guess we stop and use that setup, but I have a feeling that's not the right answer."

We all laughed.

Dave continued, "That's fine, but what if a customer wants a catapult that shoots 15 feet?"

Joe stammered, "Uh, I guess we start all over again?"

Dave just smiled and said, "You see, this is the problem in a lot of factories. You may know how to do something because over the years you discovered it by trial and error. But if you need to make adjustments or make something a little different, it's like you just started in the business."

We were all starting to get the picture now.

Russ added, "The other important thing to remember is that there are usually many ways to achieve the same result. We can set up this catapult several ways to shoot the ball ten feet. But one of the ways might shoot it ten feet more consistently. Or it may be less expensive under one set of conditions. Our DOE will give us information so we can find the *best* set of conditions to meet our objective."

I spoke up, "I think I know what you mean now. Take for instance our catalyst production. If we set our X variables up one way, the only way we know how, we usually get a certain surface area. But when our customer needed a more consistent product we didn't have a clue where to start to make the process more consistent, so we lost the opportunity. This DOE stuff will help us figure out how to do things like that?"

"Absolutely, Barry," said Dave.

Dave explained that the Blackbelts got intensive training, and he just did not have time to go into detail on DOE in half a day. He suggested we do the DOE and most of the questions would probably be answered by the exercise. He began by using the Minitab software to generate a series of test conditions for us to follow. He split us up into two teams and each team went to opposite sides of the room.

It wasn't difficult. We simply performed the DOE by changing conditions as indicated by the sheet Dave generated from the statistics software. We put on the required number of rubber bands, set the pins to the required position and pulled back the arm to the angle we needed and let the ball fly. We measured the distance with a tape measure and did each trial three times. Then we changed the conditions to the next level and repeated the shooting procedure. It took about an hour to complete all of the runs, and we took the data back to Dave. The other group was finishing up at about the same time.

Dave said, "OK, now I enter the data into the spreadsheet, and I will show you how to analyze it."

Mark said, "Hold on a minute. I haven't said anything so far, but this has been a waste of time. I don't understand what we did. We changed more than one thing at a time. You can't do that. Everyone knows if you change more than one thing you won't know what happened. We actually seem to be changing everything at the same time."

Dave smiled and said, "What you are describing is OFAT, or one factor at a time experimentation, Mark. DOE allows us to change more than one thing. This way, we can complete all of the desired conditions in less time making it more efficient, more powerful, and less expensive."

"But how do you know what is going on when you're changing everything like that?" Mark asked skeptically.

"It really is not that complex, Mark. We have a balanced model and the computer knows what we changed because the computer generated the run conditions. It is just a matter of statistics to calculate the change each variable contributed to the response."

"I just can't see the usefulness of this type of stuff in our plant, Dave. Sorry, but I don't think it applies to us." Mark was stubborn.

Dave said, "OK, here is an example. Let's say you wanted to check if a new substantially less expensive raw material could be used in your plant. How would you test that raw material today, Mark?"

"Well first we try it in the lab, but things don't scale up well here so we also bring in a truckload and just try it." Mark said.

"Do you change conditions in the plant to see how the raw material performs under different conditions, Mark?

"No, of course not, we have to hold everything constant so we can see only the effect of the raw material," Mark said defiantly.

"Well then, how do you know the raw material works or doesn't work under slightly different conditions? Maybe it works better or not at all if one of the other variables is changed slightly. Is your process so consistent that you don't have to worry about that, Mark?"

"You can't expect us to check everything! It would take forever if we had to change things one at a time while holding everything else constant," said Mark.

"Exactly, that is why DOE is preferable. You can make many changes and see the effects of all of them simultaneously." Dave was smiling. "I don't want to beat a dead horse, but this is important. What if the less expensive raw material only worked if you adjusted the process slightly from your normal conditions?"

"I'll answer that. We would never know it," I said.

Dave winked at me. "And if you tried it once and it did not work, would you ever try it again?"

"Not a chance," Howard said, shaking his head.

"You just created a sacred cow," Dave said. "The sacred cow is that your current expensive raw material is the only one that works. After a few years it becomes 'we tested all types of other raw materials and you have to use this one. It is the only one that will work.' Sound familiar?"

Joe said, "Dave? Are you sure you haven't worked here before?"

Dave laughed, "Joe, I have worked here and dozens of places just like it. That is why I say making your product is the same as making anything else when you take it down to basics."

The group was sort of stunned. I had no confidence in anything we had ever done before. I think the rest of the room felt the same way, except for Mark. He still had a sour look on his face.

Dave continued, "Well, let's proceed with the analysis of our DOE data then." He used the computer and showed us how the variables were included in the model, and the final result was an equation for each team.

"Wow, that equation is a model of our catapult process. If we had that type of information on all of our factory processes, we would be sure of finding the optimum way of making our products," Steve said, excited.

Dave smiled and said, "Exactly! Of course it will take more work in the factory, but believe me it is worth the work. Let's see how good you folks were in performing the DOE tests. We're going to validate our models."

Dave told each team there was a bet on to see which of them could set up their catapult, based on their equation, to throw the balls to six feet plus or minus one foot. Dave explained that since the catapults were different we should expect different performance and also different models.

We all huddled together. This was actually kind of fun. Based on our equation, we found that by setting the start angle all the way down at 180, the stop position at 2, the hook position at 4 and the pin position at 2, we should generate a Y response of 73 inches. That was as close as we could get to 72 inches. We got our catapult set up this way while everyone watched.

We made ten shots under the same conditions. The distance of our shots ranged from 68 inches to 78 inches.

"We have got this in the bag," said Joe.

"Move out of the way amateurs, let the pros have a shot," said Roman.

Team two completed their ten shots. Dave entered the data into the computer. He performed a capability analysis for each team and calculated the expected defect levels. Team one had a defect rate of 122,000 ppm and Team two was at 378,000 ppm.

"I told you rookies to watch out," said Henry. He was really getting into this stuff for an accountant. "I can taste that beer now."

Dave went back to the front of the room. "I know this was a little different for executive training, but it gives you an idea of what the Blackbelts will be doing. Except they will be working on real problems in your plant and winning real savings instead of beers."

Russ said, "OK, time for another Six Sigma side benefit. Did you have fun doing this?"

Bob said, "I certainly did."

Russ continued, "The side benefit is that work starts to be fun again. People fear learning new things but they really thrive on it once they get started. Especially when there is a positive atmosphere and no fear of failure."

Dave said, "We have just touched the basics of DOE, but I hope you get the general idea of how it fits into the road map of the Six Sigma process. It is not the end though. Let's take a 15-minute break and then I will tell you how we make sure the process stays under control."

As I left the room I heard Steve and Howard explaining DOE to Mark.

"This stuff is great, Mark. See how it all fits together? Find the variables in the define stage. Prove your measurements so you know you have good data. Analyze the data and select the critical variables. And then the DOE stuff will work, I know it will. We just do things now the way we have always done them. It would be unbelievable if that were the best way to do it."

Mark said, "I don't know. We have too much going on at one time to be able to use this stuff. Maybe it's OK in the lab but not in our plant."

Steve said, "Give it a chance, Mark. Dave was right when he talked about that raw material example. Think how many things we have thrown out the window because we tried it one way and it didn't work."

Howard continued, "I know one thing. We'd better do something. What are we going to tell Bob, Mark? There are no ways to save money or improve our process. I don't think the man is going to buy that."

17

Executive Training: Control

"Let's move on to the last module which is known as the control phase of the road map. Now that we know what to do, we need to do one more thing before we can sit back and take pride in our work. Who knows what that might be?" Dave said.

No one answered.

"OK, let me ask it another way then. Does it ever happen that something good works, then after a few months it slips back to the way it was?"

Mark answered, "You better believe it. We implement something in the plant and as long as my people are there watching it, we are OK. But as soon as we leave, watch out. Production just starts doing what they want and it goes back to the way it was."

"All too often the types of things you mention happen because a project is stopped before it is truly finished. In the control phase we teach people how to optimize the process and be sure it is really under control," Dave answered.

Roman continued, "Now this is where SPC is very useful. Do you use SPC here?"

Mark said, "Sure we do. We have SPC charts all over the plant."

"What things are you charting, Mark?"

"Well, color and surface area and strength level, lots of things."

"Mark, would you consider those things X variables or Y variables?"

"Let me think. Most of the charts are things we measure in the final inspection, so Y variables I guess."

"So you are controlling your process with these charts. You make changes when they indicate out-of-control behavior."

"Well, not really, Roman. See this is where our plant is different from a widget plant," Mark said.

Roman smiled, "Dave, tell them what we call those charts people call SPC charts but don't control anything with."

Dave replied, "We call them wallpaper, because all they are good for is covering the wall."

"Oh that's ridiculous," said Mark impatiently.

I spoke up, "No, Dave is right. We don't control anything with them. They are up there so our ISO inspectors and our customers think we use SPC. We don't even know what to adjust when they go out of control anyway, which is most of the time. We just set the control limits so wide that they look like they are in control."

I had always hated playing that SPC charade. We did it to impress customers and auditors. I had always convinced myself it was better than doing nothing at all. We played 'connect the dots,' that's all.

Roman said, "SPC is a valuable tool when used correctly. It is part of the control phase because it belongs at the end of the road map, not the beginning. You would be surprised at the number of companies that have a problem and expect an SPC chart to make it better. Think about it. The chart is there to tell you one thing, and that is if the process is not behaving in a normal, random manner. Has something happened that is not typical for this process? How can it tell you what variables you need to control or if your measurements are good or anything else really?"

"It makes a lot of sense now, Roman. Now I know why SPC has a bad name with a lot of people. It's not that SPC does not work, it's that people expect something from it that it cannot do," said Howard.

Roman said, "Correct. If you first identify the critical variables during the define and analyze phases, insure good measurements during the measure phase, model and predict the behavior of those variables in the improve phase, and make changes to those variables only when your control charts indicate nonrandom behavior in the control phase, you will have made monumental improvements in your process. I promise you that."

Most of us were starting to believe that Roman was right.

Dave continued, "Well that is all we had for you in this short executive training class. We really only just touched the basics. Only you can do the actual work because only you have the people with the answers. We can only help you help yourself."

Russ said, "The last piece of advice I will give you is this: if you are not going to do it right, don't do it. You have one shot at Six Sigma. People will know if you are not committed to doing it right. And this group has to walk the talk. Good luck and keep me informed."

"OK," I said. "Can our people meet on Monday at 10 o'clock in the main conference room to decide what we are going to do? That gives us the weekend to think about it."

Everyone said OK. We would make our decision on Monday.

Bob shook hands with all of us and headed out the door.

Dave said to me, "Bob's a real leader, Barry. I know the type. If he wants it to work, he won't let it fail."

"I hope you're right Dave. It's not him I'm worried about. It's some of the others. I mean if we don't do this thing right, what will happen?" I was visibly nervous.

Russ came over and assured me that everything would work out if we listened to Dave and his people. We were not the first to try this and we had a leader at the top that didn't appear to accept failure.

I thanked everyone and headed back to work.

18

The Decision

I was the first one to the conference room on Monday, and I walked in and took a seat on the far side of the table where I could see everyone as they walked in. I was sure that Mark didn't understand how important this was to the survival of our company. In charge of R&D, he was one of the keys in making this work. Quite a few of the Blackbelts would come out of his department. I could not imagine doing research any other way now.

Henry and Jimmy came in together and took seats opposite me.

"Hi, Barry," said Jimmy. "I see we got that order out to AccuChem this weekend. Thanks for pushing it through the system."

"No problem," I said. We worked overtime to get it packaged, but all we really did was delay someone else's order to get this one out on time. I was determined to get someone working on the idea of packaging the product to order like Russ suggested.

The rest of the group arrived and sat down. Bob was the last one to arrive and he took his place at the end of the table reserved for the head honcho.

Bob said, "OK, Barry, you have the floor."

"Thanks, Bob. The purpose of the meeting is to decide if we will pursue a Six Sigma implementation at this plant. If we agree it is the right thing to do, I would like to draft a plan of action and form a steering committee."

Joe, the head of our HR spoke first. "I like everything I've heard. I am not an engineer, but it made sense to me. We certainly have not been doing the amount of training we need and this is a good start."

"Thanks, Joe. Anybody else?"

Mark said, "I thought we decided not to hire any more consultants. Didn't you say you hated consultants, Bob?"

Bob clenched his teeth. "We should not use consultants unless we don't have the people in house to perform the work. And I don't hate consultants Mark, as long as we get something in return for the cost."

Mark frowned but he had to get in the last word. "It just seems to be so time-consuming, this Six Sigma approach. I am just afraid we will never get anything done. Paralysis by analysis."

"Well, Mark," Bob said. "I would rather see us solve a few problems so they don't come back than work on a hundred and solve none of them permanently."

Henry said, "I am for the program in the plant. It seems to be mainly production oriented. Finance has their hands full with the new software system. We don't have time and it should not involve us."

"What do you think, Jimmy? You haven't said anything."

Jimmy, VP sales, responded, "I would be an idiot to argue against lowering costs, improving quality, decreasing cycle time, and putting the customer number one. Count me a big yes."

"Steve and Howard?"

Howard looked at Steve. "Speaking for production, we have discussed it quite a bit and we like what we heard. I am a little concerned about making people full-time Blackbelts, but I understand why it is needed. We will have to think about who to train since we still need people to put out the fires while we get people trained."

"Jack?"

"As I said before, I don't have anything better and we need to do something. Count me in."

"OK then, it is almost unanimous. I will contact Dave and his company about getting started. Bob, this is not budgeted." I looked to Bob to get his approval.

"Well, the way I see it Barry, the savings we are going to get are not budgeted either right?"

"That is true." I continued, "I suggest we train two classes since Howard is right about needing people to keep the ship afloat. I think 20 total with 10 per class is about right for us. After that we do it ourselves. If we can start a group training in September, we will get one wave almost trained this year. We can start the next group in the first quarter of next year."

I looked around the room and everyone seemed to be OK with this.

"Alright, I will start the ball rolling. Thanks for your support. It will pay off, I am sure of that."

Everyone got up and started leaving. Bob motioned Jack and me over. "Let's talk in my office," he said.

"What do we do about Mark?" I said.

"Good question. He still does not get it. Russ said we needed full support, not just agreement, to do it," Jack said.

Bob said, looking serious, "Well, let's see how he does. I'll have a talk with him this week about it. This is too important to let one person stand in the way of our improvement. There is too much at stake."

As soon as I got back in the office, I called Dave and we set up the training schedule for the first wave. I couldn't believe that we were actually getting started on our own Six Sigma journey. The last six months had been a blur. I wondered how many other companies or plants were in the same boat as we were and if they would have as much trouble as we did getting started. Russ told me it is easier to get started with Six Sigma if you don't wait until there is significant competitive pressure to improve. The best companies see the value while they are on top and use Six Sigma to stay on top.

I suddenly remembered that I had forgotten to speak to Bob about my idea for an "event" as Russ called it. Russ was right about the defining event, when you found it you knew it. It was certainly different, but we needed to send a message to everyone that things were changing. This would certainly be the talk of the plant. I even planned to get that well-developed rumor mill working for us instead of against us for a change.

19

Setting the Stage

I spent the rest of the week walking around the plant talking to people and asking what they felt we needed to do to make the place better. I used this time to introduce the Six Sigma concept and get people's reactions. I got everything from "that sounds like just what we need" to "sounds like a waste of money to me."

I determined that the biggest problem was most people didn't see how they fit into the process. We had a lot of work to do getting the organization prepared before we actually started training people. Dave was guiding me down the correct path, but I wanted to do even more than what Dave was suggesting.

Dave had explained to me that before Blackbelt training began, we should have champion training classes for people who would have Blackbelts working for them. I understood why that was needed, but I also included union leadership and the production shift supervisors. Dave thought this was a good idea.

I had known from experience that our union would not trust Six Sigma. Not that I could blame them. They had been through a lot in the last 10 years, with layoffs and threats of closure. I needed them to believe that this was really different than anything we had attempted in the past. I needed them to believe it would work. Believing was half the battle, in my mind.

I also wrote an article in the company newsletter. It was a two-page article describing our decision to implement Six Sigma and some brief information on what it was all about. I intended to follow that up with meetings for all employees.

During one of my visits to the plant, I walked into the maintenance shop at lunchtime.

"Hi, guys, what's for lunch?"

"Not a whole lot, Barry," said a mechanic named Alan. Alan was a big guy who had been at the plant for about 10 years.

"I wanted to talk to you about something new we will be starting soon. I need your help."

"Management never listens to us. You don't need our help." Alan always said what he thought.

"Actually we do, Alan. This place is going to have to change and soon. We can't keep losing money year after year like we have been."

"Come on, Barry. This place isn't losing money. Look at all that money they spent on that office building renovation a couple years ago. They got money to buy themselves new cars every year or two. Does that look like a company that's losing money?"

"I promise you Alan, this plant is in trouble."

"Oh, don't let them fool you. They have two sets of books. Always have had two sets. What's so different now than it was ten years ago? I have heard it all before. They just want to get us ready for the contract negotiations next year and they are starting early. Try to cheat us out of our raises again."

"I can promise you that is not what this is all about." Most of the other mechanics were listening now but they weren't saying anything.

"Well, Barry, we already heard about your new program, this Six Sigma thing. It sounds pretty complicated to me. I heard it's supposed to show us how to make pigment better.

We've been doing it pretty good the same way for 35 years, why change now?"

I replied, "Because we aren't making money anymore and our competition is. That's why. We have to get a handle on costs, Alan."

"Like I said, just a way to cut some jobs and cheat us out of raises next year while upper management spends money flying all over the place and playing golf."

"Will you give it a chance, Alan?"

"I have always had an open mind, Barry. Show me it will make this place better and I will listen. We all will, right guys?" Alan turned to the other mechanics in the shop. They all nodded yes.

"Well, that is all I can ask for. I'm going to remember this when we start forming some teams and I want you on one Alan, OK?"

"I told you I would have an open mind. I want this place to succeed as much as the next guy, but management has got to change first." Alan was a tough guy.

"I agree, Alan, and I am working on that too."

I left the maintenance shop and headed back toward my office. It was going to be a tough sell to the hourly workforce, maybe tougher than I thought.

Bob was due back next week for a couple of days and I had to tell him about my idea for our kickoff event. I sure was not about to tell anyone else for fear of getting tarred and feathered. If Bob were behind it though, it would work. And I had a feeling he would back such a crazy idea. I was sure it would get everyone's attention.

I ran into Rodney on the way back to my office. Rodney was one of my favorite first-line supervisors. He was always upbeat and positive and he knew everything about this plant. He had worked every job as an operator and then every area as a foreman. I had invited him to be one of the participants in champion training.

"Pretty hot out there today, huh Rodney?"

"Man, I am getting too old for this stuff. But I love it."
Rodney had pigment on his arms and hands.

"Looks like you got into the product today."

"I was helping clean up that spill over there at the dryer. We
have got to do something about that dryer flaming out on us.
Every time it quits, I have to dump the thing and then spend
two days digging it out."

"Did you like champion training?"

"Yes, I did. Thanks for inviting me. I read the articles too.
It sounds great. Hey if GE is doing it, I like it. That company
has made me a bunch of money in the stock market." He leaned
over and whispered, "Unlike our stock."

"I know, I know. Our stock is not doing so well."

"Hey Rodney, what are the troops saying about Six Sigma?"

"Well it's like this, boss. They want to believe it, really they
do. They have just had so much stuff thrown at them the last
ten years, they don't know what to believe. They just want to
do their job and retire someday with a decent pension."

"Well, I think that is kind of sad, Rodney. Just working
your life away at some job until retirement is no way to live. I
think this will make work more exciting and satisfying for the
people that work here. Don't you think people want to be a part
of improving this place?"

"Oh, sure they do. A lot of them won't admit it, but don't
ask them to help and see them cry. What makes you think management will support Six Sigma?"

"Bob."

"The new division president?"

"Absolutely."

"If you say so. Listen, good talking to you, but I've got to
get this job order over to maintenance. Thanks for letting me
go to the class."

"Sure thing, so long, Rodney."

I watched as Rodney double-timed it over to the maintenance shop. That guy was a go-getter. We needed two dozen

more just like him. Rodney was definitely going to be an asset for our Six Sigma initiative.

I headed for the office to finish up for the day, but as I walked up the stairs I ran into Donald. Donald worked for Mark now and was one of the engineers in R&D.

"Hi, Donald, how are you?"

"Mark told us what you are trying to do, Barry. We don't need some bunch of statisticians coming in here trying to tell us what to do. If you want to know what it takes to get this place running right, all you have to do is ask me."

"Well Donald, Six Sigma is a whole lot more than just statistics and the people who will be helping us are not statisticians. They are experienced people who just happen to know how to use statistics when it is needed. Besides, you can't do everything we need to do by yourself."

"We'll see. I just don't get you, Barry. When you worked with us, everything was fine. Make you a manager and now all of a sudden, we don't know how to do anything right. I think this job went straight to your head."

"Donald, I'm sorry you feel that way, but this plant is not competitive the way we run it. We have to change to stay in business."

"Well, when your consultants come in here and screw everything up, don't come running to me to bail you out." He practically spit out the words.

"I do hope you will be a part of Six Sigma, Donald. You have a lot of valuable information, and I know you can help us a lot."

"You mean be a part of your teams and ask operators how to fix the place. Mark told us about that too. Give me a break. Operators out here don't know anything about running a chemical plant. They are the reason this place doesn't run right, because they don't follow instructions."

"I have to go, Donald. All I ask is that you have an open mind."

"My mind is always open." With that, Donald walked off muttering under his breath.

— —

Sarah was waiting for me when I walked into the office.

"Well, I got a call from a Dennis Ackerman at CMG Coatings this afternoon. They're having that problem with dispersion again."

"Ouch. I bet he was mad."

"Mad does not describe it. He says he wants all our product out of his warehouse tomorrow and he is going to buy from the competition from now on."

"Whew, let me call him and see if I can salvage things. I promised him last time this would not happen again. How have numbers been looking lately?"

Sarah replied, "Well, it is kind of hard to tell. It runs in spurts. We are still rejecting about 5 percent of our final product, but some days it's zero and others it's 10 percent."

"Are we still testing at the higher frequency?"

"Oh sure, Barry, but we can't test every bag."

"I know. Let me call him and get this over with.

I went to my office and gave Dennis a call.

"Hi, Dennis, Barry Watson here."

"Well, about time. How soon can you get that junk you call pigment out of my warehouse so I can make room for your competitor's product?"

"I am sorry, Dennis. Sarah told me what happened. Is it the same symptoms as before?"

"Worse this time. I've got three tanks full of product I can't ship because it has to be reworked. I've got shipments I have to delay. Customers are screaming down my neck. Our plant manager is involved now, that's all I needed. You guys screwed me good this time."

"I checked all our QC results and we met the new specification limits, Dennis. I don't know what happened. Could it be anything on your end?"

"Don't even try to blame us for this, Barry. This is your problem!" Dennis screamed into the phone.

"No, I didn't mean that I was trying to get out of any responsibility. I just wondered if anything was different."

"Well, we haven't had a chance to check everything. I mean after the fiasco last year, our production folks started blaming your pigment right away. You know how it is, once you have a problem they always blame the same thing again."

"I know, Dennis, we do the same thing. So you are sure it *is* the pigment?"

"I don't know. I have to tell you, we have a truckload of the competition coming in tomorrow. If the problem goes away when we switch pigment, you guys are in trouble."

"Let me send one of our folks up to help investigate, Dennis."

"Well, that would be appreciated. We have our hands full. I mean, we will get our orders out, but now that the plant manager is involved . . . I have to look out for me too. We are going to have to stick you with the plant downtime and rework costs too."

"I know, Dennis. Listen, you ever heard of something called Six Sigma?"

"Sure. We sell to Advanced Equipment, and they are pushing that on us every chance they get. I even went to one of their champion classes. All their suppliers had to go."

"What do you think of it, Dennis?"

"I like what I heard. I sure know we could apply a little more science to what we do here. Everyone thinks this process is black magic. We've got people blaming things on the phase of the moon."

"Well, we are going to start training our own Blackbelts in a month or so."

"Really, hey that's great!"

"What if I replace what you have in your warehouse and promise that one of our Blackbelts will start working on this dispersion problem next month. If it is our problem, Six Sigma will solve it. If it turns out to be your problem, we will solve it too. Either way the problem goes away. This Blackbelt will be assigned to your problem full-time. We can't afford to lose you, Dennis. What do you say?"

"Well, I like the idea of really finding out the root cause of all this and making it go away. We want to buy from you guys, but it's getting out of my league now. You know what it is like when the higher-ups get involved, the politics start, and everyone starts to play CYA."

"I would appreciate it if you could do what you can. Let me know. I appreciate you working with me, Dennis."

"Do you promise this new stuff will be OK, Barry?"

"Absolutely, I will have them retest all of it to make sure."

"Well tell you what, have a truck here tomorrow afternoon to switch it out and I will cover for you. But it better work. I think upper management will like the fact that you guys know you have a problem and have admitted it. The fact you are going the Six Sigma route will carry a lot of weight too. We have been talking about doing Six Sigma ourselves with all the pressure from customers and all."

"Well, once we get our Six Sigma initiative going, we can sure share our experiences with you, Dennis. You have been a good customer of ours for a long time."

"I will mention that to our quality manager. We may take you up on it. We know we need to do something. Things are so tough these days."

"Thanks, Dennis, that truck will be there tomorrow."

20

Our Event

I had two important things I needed to accomplish today, and both were going to be tough. First I had to tell Sarah she was going to be in the first Blackbelt wave and let Pat know he was not. More importantly, I had a meeting set up with Bob after lunch to talk about my idea to get the workforce on board with Six Sigma.

I was heading to the lab to meet with Pat and Sarah. I turned the corner and walked into Sarah's office.

"Hi, Sarah." Sarah had her back turned to me, working on her computer. Her desk was piled high with documents she was trying to get finished.

"Is Pat coming down?" I asked.

"I told him, but you might need to remind him," she said.

I picked up the phone and called Pat. The phone was ringing in his office when he walked in the door.

Pat said, "OK, what's so important you needed to talk to both of us at the same time?"

"Well, I just wanted to talk about Six Sigma," I told them.

Sarah blurted out, "So you made up your mind. You better pick me."

"Well, actually I did, Sarah." We both turned and looked at Pat.

"Hey, no fair. Why can't we both be in the first wave?" Pat complained.

I replied, "You know the answer to that Pat. The Blackbelt training is full-time and someone has to run the lab. We can let a few things slide but this is a five-month commitment. I can't put both of you in the same wave."

"Well, there better be a second wave and I better be in it."

"There will be, Pat, and I promise you will be in it."

Sarah added fuel to the fire, "That is, if we are still in business then, Pat."

Pat looked at me sympathetically.

"We will still be in business because the first wave of Blackbelts is going to make sure we are, right Sarah?" I said sarcastically.

Sarah replied, "Absolutely!"

I replied, "And that leads me to the second thing I need to tell you."

"What's that?" asked Sarah.

"I know what project I want you to work on."

"Really, what is it?"

"Sarah, I want you to work on solving our dispersion problem, the one that has been giving us fits over at CMG."

Sarah got a blank look on her face. She knew this was a very important problem but also a tough one.

Pat answered, "Now I'm kind of glad I am in the second wave."

I asked, "Sarah?" She had not said a word.

She finally responded, "I will give it my best shot, Barry, that's all I can say. That problem has been around forever. I have no idea where to start."

"All I can tell you Sarah is this: Dave says if we know how to fix the problem we don't need Six Sigma for it, we should just do it. That is why Six Sigma is sometimes referred to as the breakthrough strategy because it leads to breakthroughs. I have confidence in you. You are the best of the best, as Dave says."

Sarah stifled back a laugh and said, "I guess that makes you almost the best of the best Pat, ha, ha."

We all laughed.

"I promise I will come up with just as good a project for you, Pat."

"But what if the first wave solves all the problems before I get a chance to go to Blackbelt training?" Pat questioned.

I looked over my glasses at Pat. "Do you really think we can solve all of the problems at this place in five months?"

Pat looked down sheepishly, "Oh yeah, for a minute I forgot where I worked."

I headed out the door and I could hear Pat and Sarah talking about Six Sigma. I heard Pat tell Sarah that he knew she would get to go first all along. I knew one of the reasons Pat was anxious to join the training was the fact that a Six Sigma Blackbelt could immediately land a job in another company. Once you knew the methodology, it could be applied any-where. There were a lot of companies looking for Blackbelts. To a Six Sigma company it was like hiring an expert problem solver off the street that already knew how your company oper-ated. It was a great advantage in the hiring process to know what you were getting.

Roman had told me that you had to take care of your Blackbelts to keep them. Russ was giving his Blackbelts stock options and a bonus at the end of training. I wanted to do some-thing special for our Blackbelts too, but I had to discuss it with Bob and find out what was available. We certainly did not want to lose them after we had invested so much time and money in training them.

I also knew that Pat was ambitious and he saw this as a career-enhancing move. It was pretty common knowledge at GE that being a successful Blackbelt would get you noticed at cor-porate. It was really smart to tie Six Sigma to career progression.

Downtown, I took the elevator to the second floor and walked down to Tamara's desk. Tamara saw me coming and smiled at me.

"He's waiting for you, Barry, go right on in."

"Thanks, Tamara."

Bob was sitting behind his desk, which was piled high with papers. He pulled his glasses off and walked over to shake my hand.

"Hi, Barry, how's the plant running?"

"Just normal I'm afraid."

"Well, normal does not sound that bad."

"Our version of normal can be pretty bad. What you can get used to over time is unbelievable."

"It can't be as bad as last month, right?" Bob started to sound worried.

"Oh no, last month was really bad. This month we will make budget."

"How is Six Sigma going?" He sounded enthusiastic.

"That's what I really wanted to talk to you about today."

"Are there any problems?"

"No, not really. I have just spent a lot of time talking with people and they just can't see what we see. They have had so much thrown at them the last ten years. We tried the Crosby program eight years ago and it was good but it didn't change things. Then we brought in that consulting group a few years later and formed a lot of teams and ended up cutting jobs instead of fixing anything. Now everyone is comparing Six Sigma to those programs. They just don't believe in what we're doing."

"Any ideas on how to get people on board, Barry?"

"I'm glad you asked." I had a look of mischief on my face.

Bob bit his lip and said, "Maybe I shouldn't have asked."

"Russ says we need to do something that will make people sit up and take notice. A defining event he calls it. The moment where people have to say, 'this place is changing.' "

"So what do we have to do?"

"Here is my idea, Bob. People are not going to believe this company wants to change unless they see it happening first. I say we convince them by doing something so dramatic it will be the talk of the plant."

"What can we possibly do that will have that effect, Barry?"

"Sell off all the executive company cars." I held my breath and looked for any reaction that might tell me I was about to get fired.

Instead Bob smiled and pointed his finger at me while nodding his head. I could tell the wheels were turning.

I asked, "Well?"

"I like it. I can't tell you how many people complain about those cars. They really are a sore point. I have never experienced anything like it."

I explained to Bob about how the cars were bought around the time there were cutbacks. He understood better when he heard the other side of the story.

"I know it's not that much money saved, but it sends a great message."

"Oh, you're absolutely right about that, Barry. The message is clear. We are changing and we are starting at the top."

"I also like the fact that there is some sacrifice at the top since most people blame our problems on management anyway. I think we need to say, 'management will give up their cars until we get our plant profitable.' It has a good message," I said.

"I really like it," Bob replied.

"Well, I had another idea about the cars too, Bob."

"Well, let's hear it. The first one was pretty good."

"Instead of just getting rid of them, let's auction them off at the plant. Let the employees bid on them. We can set a minimum bid so we get our money out of them. Just think about it. Every time someone sees someone driving one of those company cars to work, it will remind them of how management took the first step to change."

"That sounds like a winner too, Barry."

"One last thing though, Bob. The VPs will have to act like they bought into the idea. They can't go around telling people they were made to do it. People have to believe management really wants this place to succeed, and they are willing to sacrifice personally to do it."

"I can tell you have thought a lot about this, Barry. I can promise you no one working for me will say a negative word in public about those cars being taken away, uh, I mean given up voluntarily." I could tell Bob was serious about that.

"Thanks Bob, when can I start the rumor? This is one message we want to start as a rumor so people will talk about it. It won't take long. I promise you it will be the talk of the plant. Then we can post an official notice. Purchasing always posts auction notices for old company equipment anyway."

"Tell you what, Barry. I will call a meeting with my direct reports tomorrow morning and tell them, so hold off on the rumor until tomorrow after lunch. And I have an idea of how to say it. Tell people the company is selling off the cars in order to pay for the Six Sigma training. Management thinks Six Sigma is so important to the success of this company that we are sacrificing our cars to pay for the training. That ought to open a few eyes, huh? And it really is the truth."

"Boy, I like the way you think, Bob. This is just what we need to set the stage. Plus we save a lot of money, which we really should be doing anyway."

Bob got up and patted me on the shoulder as I walked out of his office. We said good-bye and I walked out to my truck as high on life as I had been in a long time. This was going to be fun. We were going to save our plant and it was going to be fun doing it. Would wonders never cease? I could not wait to tell someone, but I had to wait until tomorrow afternoon. I also had a good idea who to tell first, my good buddy Lou from operations.

21

The Big Rumor

The next day at work I could hardly wait until after lunch. I had called Bob that morning and he assured me that his end of the deal would be upheld that morning. I walked into the plant to catch Lou in his office, not that it would be hard to do that at lunchtime. He was right where I thought he would be, finishing up his lunch.

"Hey Lou, how is the P-101 run going?"

Lou looked up from his lunch. "Pretty good, Barry. Of course we could do better but I'm not complaining," Lou mumbled.

"Have you heard the latest?"

"About what?" Lou gave me a scared look. Lou was only five years or so away from retirement and anything that happened that would interfere with that made him very nervous.

"I heard from a reputable source that the executive staff are going to sell off the company cars to pay for the Six Sigma training."

I thought Lou was going to choke on the piece of pound cake he was chewing.

"Holy smoke! You must be kidding. Sell those new cars?"

"That's what I heard."

"You are sure about this? Who told you?"

"Well, I can't say, Lou, but it's a reliable source. I promise you that."

"Wow. Maybe things are really going to change around here after all. Who are they going to sell the cars to?"

"I heard they were going to auction them off here at the plant like they do with all the old equipment."

"Really? Man, I sure would love to get my hands on that Chrysler Concorde Steve drives."

"Well, you might get a shot at it. I hear they plan on doing it next week."

"But why are they really doing it, Barry?"

"Well, Lou, it's no secret this plant has been losing money and we need to cut costs. Management really likes Six Sigma and thought this would be a good way to pay for it since it was unbudgeted. They finally figured out that things need to change and the place to start was at the top."

"Man that does it! It's about time we started doing something to get this place back on track. Hey, count me in on that Six Sigma stuff. I don't know much about it, but I will help any way I can. I need five more years out of this place. Shoot, I might hang around if we start making money again."

"I appreciate that, Lou. Have a good day."

I walked out the door and stopped just outside. I heard Lou pick up the phone and dial. "Hey Willard, you ain't gonna believe what I just heard!"

I continued walking down the hall, smiling. I knew I could count on good old Lou to get the word out. I hoped everyone had the same reaction as he did to the news.

I had been in my office two hours when the phone rang. It was Sarah on the phone.

"Have you heard about the cars, Barry?"

"No, what cars, Sarah?" I played dumb.

"Well, Pat and I heard that the big shots are auctioning off their cars to pay for Six Sigma and we are going to get a chance to buy them."

"You must be kidding. Our VPs aren't going to give up those cars." I was leading her on.

"No really, I heard it from a reliable source."

"Who, Sarah?"

"Well, the storeroom delivery girl heard it from maintenance when she was delivering a pump. The maintenance department supposedly got it from the union hall. The union is saying the company is finally waking up. I'm surprised you don't know anything about it."

"Well, it sure sounds good to me. I'm glad something is happening that's going to save us some money."

"I still can't believe it myself. I sure hope it is true though. It sure needs to be done. The union is saying Six Sigma must really be important to get these VPs to sell off their cars to pay for it."

"Keep me informed, OK?"

"No problem."

I shook my head. This was going too good. It had taken all of two hours to make it from Lou to the union to the lab. I called Bob to see how the meeting went this morning.

"Hi, Tamara, it's Barry. Is Bob in?"

"Sure, Barry, I'll patch you through."

Bob picked up his phone, "Hi Barry."

"Well, Bob, the rumor is alive and well. I told one person in production two hours ago and it made it from there to maintenance to the storeroom to the union to the lab in two hours. Everyone in the plant will know by tomorrow.

"What are they saying?"

"They are saying Six Sigma must be important for the VPs to sell off their cars. They also think maybe the company really is ready for a change this time."

"Wow, that is good news."

"How did the meeting go?"

"Well, it was pretty quiet at first. When I told them what we were going to do, you could have heard a pin drop. Then they all started to buy in on it. They are all pretty scared about losing their jobs if we can't turn this place around. I really was happy to see their reaction. I think it is going to work out fine. I told them that once we got profitable again, we would look at replacing the cars or adjusting their pay level to account for it."

"Wow. That sounds great Bob. I sure didn't expect that reaction."

"Think about it. Would you volunteer to give up something of value? Most people would not. If it is across the board though, they can understand the need for it."

I answered, "Yeah, that makes sense. Gotta run now but I will keep you informed, Bob."

"Please do, Barry. Anything you need, let me know."

I hung up the phone and went out to check on things in the plant.

22

People Really Do Care

Jason Hodges was standing next to Billy Montgomery and a few others in the clock alley waiting for the time clock to hit 7 a.m. so they could go to work. They were all mumbling to themselves, reading the notice, when Carl, the union chief, walked up.

"What's the company gone and done to us now," Carl said sarcastically as he walked up toward the bulletin board. "Gonna lay a bunch more of us off to save money again, I bet."

The bulletin board in the clock alley was where all of the important company messages were posted, not that people didn't know through the rumor mill first. But posting it made it official.

"You ain't gonna believe this one, Carl," said Jason.

"I'd believe anything this company would do," said Carl. He peered over the top of Jason's shoulder.

Carl started reading the notice and was unconsciously reading out loud, "Company is . . . losing money and . . . Six Sigma and to . . . reduce costs we will . . . auction off . . . company cars. What! Auction off the company cars!" he practically shouted.

"That's what it says, Carl. Says right there in black and white the auction will be on Wednesday."

Carl replied sarcastically, "Must be some kind of trick. Union negotiations are coming up soon and this is just a way to make us think they are losing money so they don't have to give us a raise."

"I don't think so, Carl," said Billy. "I gotta friend lives close to Henry and he said Henry was out shopping for a new car cause the company was selling his to raise money to pay for improvements."

"Yeah Carl, don't you trust nothing? It looks like the company has finally come to its senses about making some changes to get this place right."

Carl replied, "Well. I'm just a cautious guy. Seen a lot of tricks in my time in this business." Carl looked up at the crowd that had gathered behind him. "I'll tell you one thing though. If this company sells those cars . . . maybe . . . maybe things are starting to change."

"Yeah, I think so," said someone from the back of the crowd.

"Hey, how much you think they are gonna ask for 'em?" came another voice from the rear. "My wife needs a new car."

"You guys better punch the clock and get to work," said Carl. "Or you won't have a job to pay for food much less a new car. I don't believe anything I read and only half what I see when it comes to management." Carl punched his card in the clock and then stuck the card in his slot.

As he walked to the shop, Billy thought to himself that it was a good day to get some work done. Maybe he'd clean out that mess in the storage area everyone had been putting off. It had showed up on the housekeeping list for three months now.

23

The Blackbelts

The time had come to select the ten Blackbelts that would form the first wave. I thought about what Dave had told me about selecting the right people. The selection of the Blackbelt trainees was critical, he said. They needed certain traits to be effective.

Russ said it was hard to tell who the superstars were going to be so don't be too critical, but there were guidelines to help select the best people. Russ said above all people had to have the desire to promote change in the organization. Find those that are respected by their peers and those that could be team players.

Russ had warned me not to try and make a Blackbelt out of someone who did not have the necessary qualifications or show any desire in the first training sessions. He told me that there would be enough going on without trying to drag someone through the process that did not belong.

Russ usually found that some of the champions would be hesitant to give up their best people. A champion who did not want to give you one of their best people was not on board. Don't let them get away with it, he told me. Demand the best and pull out the big guns if you have to. Nothing was more important than picking the right people.

I was poring over my list of potential Blackbelts when Pat came in.

"What are you studying?"

"It just happens to be a list of Blackbelt candidates," I replied.

"Got any good ones on the list?"

"Well, Russ warned me that this would happen and guess what? You sure can tell who is committed to Six Sigma based on the people the champions are offering to be in the first wave."

"Mark gave me two people out of R&D like I asked, but you could not have picked two worse people if you had tried. And I think he tried."

Pat peered over my shoulder. "OK, what's wrong with this guy Donald. He seems like an OK kind of guy."

I rolled my eyes up at Pat and said, "He has managed to upset almost every single person in operations at least twice. He's a know-it-all and won't listen to anyone. He already told me he thinks Six Sigma is a waste of time and he thinks he can solve any problem by himself. Mark suggested him because he doesn't have much to do these days."

"Is that all?" laughed Pat patting me on the back.

"Yeah, right," I replied sarcastically.

"Now the other one, Julie, maybe she's OK but she only started here three months ago. I'm not sure she has enough experience. She barely knows her way around the plant. And maintenance wants Ed to be trained. I've worked with him before but he is lacking people skills."

Pat asked, "Well does Ed want to be a Blackbelt?"

"Absolutely, he was in my office the day after we posted the announcement. He wants to contribute. I think I'll discuss Ed and Julie with Russ, but no way I'm taking Donald. He wouldn't let the trainer talk."

"You're probably right."

"I know I am. Now Sarah is the opposite. She gets along with everyone and has been on every team we ever formed. People respect her because they know she is a hard worker. She values people's opinions. That's the type of person I need, and that's the type of person I'm gonna get."

I turned back to the list of people in front of me. I needed 10 people for my first wave of training. The way I saw it I had six good people on the list, three 'maybes,' and one 'absolutely not.' I had asked Mark to give me one of his all-stars, one of his younger engineers, Tim. Tim fit the Blackbelt model perfect. I picked up the phone and called Bob.

"Hi, Bob. It's Barry. I expected your voice mail."

"Well, I do work sometimes, Barry," Bob chuckled. "What's up?"

"Well, Mark is still not on board. Of all the good people he had to choose from for Blackbelt training, he gave me Donald." I was still upset.

"Donald! You're kidding, Barry." Bob was laughing. "That guy is lucky he has a job. I get calls about him all the time."

"I know, Bob. Anyway, I want Tim in the first class."

"You got it. Anything else I can do for you?" he said sincerely.

"Nope, that would do it." I hung up the phone and waited for the call from Mark.

Instead of a phone call, twenty minutes later I heard Mark practically running down the hall towards my office. I smiled and looked peacefully at the door.

Mark charged into my office. He stood there red-faced with his hands on his hips. "Who do you think you are? Going over my head!" he bellowed.

"Why don't you come in and shut the door, Mark," I replied calmly.

"I just got a call from Bob informing me that I was to give you Tim instead of Donald for your Blackbelt class. Tim is up to his neck in environmental projects. I can't spare him. Donald is a better choice anyway. He has a background in statistics and knows this place backwards and forwards."

"Well, first of all I told you up front that I wanted Tim and second that I would not accept Donald. Why don't you just give Tim's projects to Donald?" I inquired calmly.

"Because Donald has his own work!"

"But if Donald has so much more experience then he can handle a lot more than a rookie engineer like Tim." I had him and he knew it.

"Well, Donald has to . . . well . . . he just doesn't . . ." Mark just sighed.

"Donald doesn't what Mark? Doesn't work well with people. You knew my main requirement was to have someone who worked well with people." I made a deliberate effort to remain calm.

"I think Donald would make a good Blackbelt. Anyway, aren't you supposed to be teaching people how to do this Six Sigma stuff anyway? If you can't teach Donald then what good is it?"

"We can't erase Donald's past history, Mark. Maybe later down the road we will try him as a Blackbelt, but not now. We have too much riding on this. His inclusion in the class would send the wrong message." I was confident in this.

"Well, I guess it's no good me telling you my problems since you will just go over my head, right?"

"If that's what it takes," I replied. Boy I was glad Bob had come to work as president of our division.

"Well, since I have no choice. But I am going to tell Bob that if we don't meet our department objectives this year it's your fault." Mark stormed out and slammed the door.

I shook my head. I had bigger fish to fry. I had my man and we were one step closer to getting something done.

— ▲ ▲ —

That afternoon, I reviewed my candidates with Russ and Dave, and they agreed Donald could not be in the first wave. They thought Ed could be helped with his people skills. And both reminded me that it was not a requirement to be an expert in production to be a good Blackbelt. Julie's qualifications were excellent so she was in the first class too.

The champions that had Blackbelts working for them met to discuss project selection and problem statements. It went pretty well except Howard and Mark had a problem with Rodney being in the first Blackbelt class. They did not dislike Rodney, but he did not have a college degree. He had worked his way up through the production ranks.

I told them they did not have to worry about Rodney. Sure, his math skills might not be up to par with the engineers, but he made up for it with enthusiasm, and people respected him. Dave told us in champion training that other Blackbelts would help those with weak math skills and it was not a major problem. Being a Blackbelt was a lot more than math and computers and statistics. I held out for Rodney and was happy to have him in the class.

I reviewed the projects; if we could solve them, it would really help out the plant. I believed in the Six Sigma system, really I did. But there was a little voice in the back of my head that had a hard time accepting that these ten people could solve these ten problems in five months. We had been realistic in the scope of the projects, but in most cases we did not even have a clue where to start. I tried hard not to show my weak side and I don't think anyone knew I was worried. Not only was the plant at stake, but my personal reputation was on the line. If Six Sigma did not work, I just could not see myself continuing to work at HPZ.

24

The Auction

When I pulled into my parking place at the plant at 6:45 a.m., the six company cars up for sale were proudly parked in the area in front of the building. The minimum bids were posted on the windows and some of them would be a good deal if they went for the minimum.

I watched from a distance as every single employee who was going to and from work went over to check out the cars. Everyone. You would have thought they were giving away gold watches or something. People looked inside the windows, kicked the tires, and wandered about talking to each other. It was almost as if everyone was whispering. I went closer to try and hear.

Jake was a senior operator in the plant and he had just gotten off the midnight shift. He was checking out a Nissan Maxima that Henry had driven up until yesterday. He looked under the car, pushed it up and down, and tried to look under the hood but the car was locked.

"Hi there, Jake," I said. "Thinking about making a bid on this one?"

Jake looked up at me through his dirty safety glasses. "Maybe."

"Well, what do you think about management selling off the cars?" I watched his reaction as he sized up the question.

"Well . . . I see it like this, Barry. I have seen this place throw away so much money in my 35 years here I could not believe this place has been losing money like they said. I mean just last year we built that new production line and the thing has hardly run a week. Now I see these cars here for sale. And I know how these managers loved their cars. And I gotta say we must be hurting for cash. I mean . . . I am worried about this place for the first time in 35 years."

I couldn't help but crack a smile. "Well, it's true and I am here to say we can get things back on track if we all work together."

"Ya know . . ." Jake shook his head and looked at me. "I don't really need this job, but I like to work. But my son and and my brother's boy Josh . . . they got a family, and young people these days don't know what it means to save for a rainy day. Heck, they owe more than I own. But they need these jobs. And I would like to do whatever I can to help them out."

"Well that's really great Jake. And we need your help . . . believe me we need it." I was sincere about that. Jake knew more about how this place really operated than I would ever know. "You going to go home and get some sleep?"

"Nope. Got some stuff to do in town first."

I saw Lou over next to Steve's Chrysler Concorde.

"Hey, Lou. That's the one huh?" I yelled over to him.

"Quiet, Barry. If these other guys know I want it they will bid high just to keep me from getting it."

"Sorry."

"What do you think this one will go for?" Lou leaned over and whispered.

"How should I know. What do you think people's overall reaction is to all this?"

Lou backed up a step. "People don't know what to think. Carl told the union it was a trick and that this would never happen. He's even telling people the VPs were tired of these and this is a way to get new cars for themselves."

"You have got to be kidding me, Lou."

"Nooo . . . you know Carl as well as I do. But people are not buying it. They are as tired of his ranting as we are. We might get a proactive leader in the union if he keeps it up."

"Well, that would be a hidden reward I would say. So overall the effect is positive."

"Absolutely."

As I walked back to my office, I wished we could leave the cars out front forever. Selling the cars was giving us the chance to prove to people we were ready to change. But if we did not take advantage of this opportunity to really change things, I knew we would never gain the trust of the employees again. I felt like this was our final chance to turn things around at HPZ.

25

Blackbelt Training:
Define and Measure

The ten Blackbelts and their champions were all assembled in the training room. Another cost I had forgotten to include was for the ten new laptops and software. That had cost us $2000 per Blackbelt, but we would be able to use the computers for our future Blackbelt classes. My neck was sticking out a little farther each day.

Roman was teaching the define and measurement modules this week and we had Bob and Jack come in to kick off the meeting.

"I wanted to personally thank each of you for being a part of this Blackbelt class," said Bob. He had cancelled a business trip to be here this morning, and you could tell the Blackbelts were impressed that the division president would show up for something like this.

He continued, "We have a lot of work to do in a short period of time and your champions and I have faith in your abilities. Please call me personally if you need anything, and I mean anything." He was serious.

"The same goes for me," said Jack.

I knew Jack meant what he said but he just did not have the charisma or leadership abilities of Bob. I knew without Bob we would be in trouble.

"OK," I said as Bob and Jack left the room, "let's get started." I intended to sit in on as much of the training as I could, but I would not be able to be present for all of it. "Roman, the floor is yours."

"Great. First thing is relax. We are going to have fun although it will be a lot of hard work." Roman started his PowerPoint presentation and the students followed along in their books. I slipped out the back door.

At lunchtime, I made my way back to the class. Dave suggested we bring lunch in each day. He said this was a nice reward for the Blackbelts, but it really kept them from going back to their offices and getting swamped with work. They needed to be as full-time in training as possible. If they went back to their offices for lunch, some would get hit with problems and some would be late and no one would be as fresh for the afternoon session. I heard a couple of the Blackbelts talking as I came up.

Sarah said, "Julie, you need to go to Mark and make him define the project and the goals better. It's way too broad. 'Improve packaging.' What does that mean? How will you know when you have done it? You heard what Roman told us about defining the problem well."

"I know, Sarah, but I have only been here three months and Mark makes me nervous. Plus I don't think he likes Six Sigma very much."

"You have to stand up for yourself. No one else is going to."

"I know, its just something I have to get prepared for," Julie said nervously.

I felt sorry for Julie. I knew what it felt like to be new and unsure of what to do. That was going to change, though.

As I walked up to them I said, "Hey Julie, why don't you and I go together to Mark and sort it out. It was really my idea for the packaging project so it's partly my fault."

"That would be great, Barry. I really appreciate it."

Over lunch I spoke with Roman about his work. He told me that the Six Sigma training business was growing quickly, maybe too quickly. Some of the companies were now promoting that clients send a few people at a time to train together with employees of other companies instead of hosting their own training.

I asked, "What's wrong with that?"

"It isn't really wrong, but it prevents a company's Blackbelts from interacting with each other. When the students in a class all work for the same company, they develop a kind of team spirit. They talk about their feelings and problems, and work together. They are not alone when they go back into the plant after their week of training. Best of all, they learn about the projects their classmates are working on. I can't begin to tell you how many projects are solved from something another student said that sparked an idea."

I said, "Oh, I see what you mean. If the class is composed of people from many different companies, there is no real common goal for the group."

"Right, Barry. The team dynamics are hard to put a price on. It is not uncommon for a corporation to send people from different divisions, but they still share a common goal. They work for the same company."

"Companies need to be careful who they pick to do the training," Roman said. "All of our trainers grew up working in the business world and have a good feel for what it takes to succeed. There is so much more to Six Sigma than the statistics and the tools."

"What do you mean, Roman?"

"Things like champions who are not on board, Blackbelt selection, projects that get bogged down, roadblocks set up by production, and lots of other things. There are a lot of things that can derail a Six Sigma initiative."

"I see what you mean. Just getting an opportunity to try Six Sigma was hard enough. I hate to think what it would be like if you guys and Russ were not here to help us out now."

Roman added, "I just don't want to see Six Sigma get a bad reputation. It is a great business initiative. But it takes time and effort and experience."

I could see how experience made a difference. "How is our training going so far?"

"You have a great group here. All of them are sharp and motivated and want to be here. They didn't even complain too much when they heard I give them homework each night."

"You give homework?"

"It's essential to the learning process, Barry. They think they understand the concepts until they get home and try to do it by themselves. Then they try to figure it out. Next morning we review the homework problems. It makes it stick." He pointed to his head.

"You are the expert, Roman. Let me get back and see what's happening in the plant. Let's go to dinner one night this week."

"Sounds good, Barry. Let me know what night."

The first week after training, there was more activity in our plant than I had ever seen. Each of the ten Blackbelts had formed a team. That meant about 60 additional people in the plant were team members and the team members were learning Six Sigma as well. People were questioning everything. It was great. And the best part was we didn't miss one deadline or make one less pound of product because the Blackbelts were not doing their regular jobs. Other people just took up the slack.

One of the Blackbelts, Richard, had come tearing into my office after a meeting with his team to develop their process map. Richard's project was to reduce raw material costs. He found out from the operator on his team that we no longer used a spray to prevent dusting on one of our bulk products stored outside. Even though the instructions said to use it and we had it in the storeroom, it was not being used.

The operator said that the person that used to do that task had their position eliminated a couple of years ago. No one had been assigned that duty. The operator said she would be happy to do it if they wanted her to.

Richard said that he had no idea how much raw material was being blown away or what it was worth, he was just amazed that he could find something so soon just by asking the right questions. He was trying to figure out how to quantify it now.

I was sitting at my desk one afternoon a couple of weeks later when Sarah came in with a handful of graphs and statistics.

"We can't test for dispersion, Barry. How am I supposed to fix something we can't even test for?" She was waving the papers at me.

"What do you mean, Sarah?"

"I did a gage R&R on the dispersion test like they taught us. Blind samples with all the technicians and here are the results. She pointed to the papers."

I looked at the graphs and numbers. "I really don't know what I am looking at here, Sarah."

"OK, well here is the range chart. See how much difference we have between people and even the same sample? The control chart limits are way too wide. We only have two distinct categories. Our ANOVA table says we can't really tell the difference between the different samples and our part-to-part variation is only 25 percent. Can you believe that, 25 percent." She put her hands on her hips.

"Wow. I wish I knew what you were talking about. You learned all that last week?"

Sarah continued talking faster and faster. "Oh, that's just a small part of what we learned. I showed these numbers to John in research and he said no way the test is that bad. He developed the test himself you know, and he says he can always get the right number. He's on my team, you know. He really needs to go through Blackbelt training. He really does."

"Slow down a little, Sarah. You are making me short of breath."

"You just don't know what this means, Barry. The reason we have dispersion complaints is because we can't tell the difference between good and bad. Even if we say it's good, it can be bad. The test is pathetic. I'd like to make John run some blind samples and see just how good he is."

"Sounds like a breakthrough to me, Sarah."

"A breakthrough. Are you nuts? If I don't have a good test, I can't even analyze the data I have, and I sure can't perform a DOE during the improve phase. I have to fix the test now, but that's not what this is all about, Barry. It's about fixing the product. Even if we can test accurately for it, you can't 'test the quality in,' remember? You have to manufacture quality into the product."

I smiled at Sarah. "Looks like you have your work cut out for you."

She just smirked at me and grabbed her papers and walked out. I could tell she was intensely proud of her discovery. I also decided I needed to spend a little more time in the training classes, I was falling way behind. I knew she was right on her statistics, but I . . . I couldn't believe what I was thinking. Russ told me that a lot of people resented Six Sigma because it took away their chance to be the big shot.

For a lot of years, I played the hero role. People asked me to make the big decisions and I kind of liked it, made me feel important. Sarah knew more than I did about this, which was clear. She also did not need me to tell her what to do, and as a matter of fact she didn't even ask me like she usually did. Who would have believed it would be me that would be the first to think like this?

26

Blackbelt Training: Analyze

It was now exactly one month after we had started training the first Blackbelt class. Each Blackbelt had utilized the three weeks after training to work on the required elements of their project. All of the Blackbelts had to give update presentations on their projects for the class and their champions.

As I listened to the updates I was amazed. It was funny, but the person I was sure would be a perfect Blackbelt, Tim from R&D, seemed to be farthest behind. He was working on a critical project too, surface area, and he had not even completed his gage R&R on the test.

Our representative from maintenance, Ed, whose people skills I was worried about, was the talk of the plant. It seemed his team loved him. He brought doughnuts to their meetings, respected their opinions, and had people begging to be included on his team. Turned out he was a natural born leader who had never been asked to lead a team before. Go figure. It just went to show you had to give people a chance to prove themselves. Don't judge a book by its cover.

The other Blackbelt from R&D, Julie, was doing great, too. She even contacted a local company on her own that specialized in running a warehouse, to learn more about handling and storing lots of different products. Roman had mentioned in his class that you needed to benchmark against the "best in class" not just the business you were in. Julie jumped on the bandwagon, and as a bonus it wasn't costing us a dime. The warehouse company volunteered to put one of their people on her team just because she asked them for help. She had intrigued them so much about what she was doing that they just wanted to know what Six Sigma was all about.

The rest of the group was doing well, too, but there were problems that had to be addressed. Paula was next to present her finance project to the class and I knew what she was going to say.

"Well, I know I am behind on the work, but Henry insisted that I help on the ERP software startup. I told him I was supposed to be full-time as a Blackbelt and I was falling behind, but you know how far I got with that."

I looked over at Dave, who was teaching the second module, and he shook his head. Henry was one of the weak champions I was warned about. Every deployment had at least one, I was told. The type that doesn't walk the talk. I had to have a meeting with him and it wasn't going to be pretty. I could tell Paula was upset that she was behind.

Rodney, our production supervisor, was doing great. He needed help on the statistics and computer work, but Richard was a whiz at this stuff and was helping him through it. Rodney was a people person and that was his strength. His team was fully behind him and he was making good progress on the drying project.

"Our team is really working hard," said Rodney. I know our project is not as high-profile as some others but until you have had to shovel up a pile of dust as high as your head, you don't know what I mean."

We all laughed at Rodney. He kept the Blackbelts entertained with his sense of humor.

Rodney continued, "We did learn quite a bit though. I have to tell you the group did not think much about the PFMEA at first. But once we got started and they saw we really wanted to hear what they had to say, I could not shut 'em up. We were there for three hours. We came up with tons of stuff to look at."

All in all, Dave thought we were on track and pleased with our progress. The analyze phase was the most concentrated in statistics and that can be mentally draining. I sat through some each day and it was challenging, but the training material was excellent. You could tell that someone other than a statistician had developed it. The examples and homework were all "real world," there were flow diagrams that showed you which statistics test to apply, and it actually made sense. I understood what Denise had said now about it sticking with you.

I could see the confidence building in the Blackbelts. They were not afraid to make decisions because they were comfortable backing up their claims with statistical evidence.

James, who worked in engineering, had some interesting things going on with his project. He was working on the residue level of P-101, our largest selling product. This was the product we had tested in 1985 with the baghouse that failed because the residue went too high. I was watching this project very closely. James had gotten the data from the test in 1985 and analyzed it statistically using ANOVA, or analysis of variance. He found at a 95 percent confidence level, that there was no difference in the residue level before, during, or after the test. Sure the number was higher, but when you took into account all of the variation from testing and the breakdowns and other parameters, the levels were the same. I mean, if the numbers were all exactly the same, now that would be suspicious. Bill, who was responsible for running the test in 1985, was retired now, but James had called him and he was attending the team meetings. He was a big help to the team because he had so much valuable experience.

Dave explained that people just have a hard time with cause and effect. They want to find a reason for everything that happens. No matter how small a difference is obtained, they develop a theory, usually one that fits their preconceived notions.

Dave did an example by sampling colored balls from a box, and it was amazing the differences you could get between people. It had nothing to do with people's techniques, only random variability. There were a certain percentage of red balls in the box, but sometimes you would get a few and other times a whole bunch. It was really great to see random variability demonstrated that way.

I thought about what it would have been like if I had agreed to teach the training like Jack had wanted. Talk about the blind leading the blind. Jack even laughed about it now after sitting in on some of the presentations from the Blackbelts. The only problem I had with Six Sigma was that it was nearly impossible to understand what it was all about until you actually did it. It took a leap of faith, or in our case a death threat from the competition, to get started.

I was surprised to find out our VP of research, Mark, was even starting to come around a little. He was not openly supporting Six Sigma, but his behind-the-scenes bad-mouthing had stopped. I knew what had done it. John and Mark had worked together for years, and Sarah made a bet with John, the research lab manager, that he could not tell the difference between samples of varying dispersion quality if they were submitted to him blind. John was confident because he had developed the test.

She really had nothing to lose because if John had been able to test them accurately, she would have solved her test problem. It would have been a training issue most likely. She was convinced, though, that John was guilty of unintentional scientific bias. And boy was she right. His results were poorer than the technicians' in the lab and Mark was there to witness it.

Fortunately, Sarah had a chemist from CMG on her team that knew a great test for paint dispersion. They were running the R&R studies on it this month in our lab and at CMG. Dennis, at CMG, was thrilled to have someone from his plant learning Six Sigma. He even dropped the claim for downtime in his plant because of the poor-quality shipment.

We were making real progress, but Dave said to wait until we started the improve phase. We would see what was really happening but we should also expect some resistance from production. We would be stepping on some toes, he said.

27

Blackbelt Training: Improve

I wasn't able to spend a lot of time in the training classes during this module, which really upset me. Dave and Roman had whet my appetite for DOE during the executive training. They did use the Statapult, but they also had some other practical examples.

Paula was a little upset that her project just did not lend itself to a DOE, so she helped Tim with his. This way she was able to fulfill her qualifications for certification and get some practical experience.

Dave was also teaching this module, and he explained that the real goal of a Blackbelt project was to solve the problem, not to try and use all of the tools. If the project could be solved in the define and measurement stages, great. Solve it and start working on something else. They only demanded that all the tools were used during training so the Blackbelts had some practical experience.

There were quite a few experiments that had to be run in the next three weeks. Dave explained that it was acceptable to put some of them off until the fourth module if you had to. He understood that we still had a plant to run.

The problem was that the plant had orders and really did not want to take a chance on doing something that would slow it down. But if they had their way, we would never run the tests. I was late for a meeting in production to discuss running Tim's DOE on the #1 rotary kiln.

— —

"Come on in, Barry. Everyone is here now," said Tim.

"Tim, why don't you explain what you want to do for all of us," said Mark, who was starting to act like a Six Sigma convert.

"Everyone knows that my project is to better control surface area. This affects all of our products, and we really just take what we get off the production line. All of our past history pointed to the kilns not having that much effect, but our team thinks otherwise. We believe that the way we run that part of the plant is critical to obtaining consistent surface area."

Our plant manager, Charlie, replied, "While I know your statistics may tell you that, Tim, there are some things only experience can teach and this is one of them. Start messing around with that kiln and we could be in real trouble."

"I know your reservations, Charlie, but this DOE is going to be a screening factorial and we are going to just manipulate the variables within the range where we already run. In other words, we don't intend to break a lot of new ground. Here is the test setup."

"I don't understand, Tim," said Steve, who was VP of manufacturing and Charlie's boss. "If you are not planning on doing anything different how can you learn anything?"

"Well first, Steve, I was lucky that the surface area test is a good one so I was able to use regression analysis and correlate the data we have been getting for the last year to all of the variables. This allowed me to reduce the number of variables down to a workable few. It's pretty interesting too."

Tim was speaking with a lot of confidence. He continued, "It seems that the temperature is important, but the biggest thing I see is the rotation speed and oxygen content of the off gasses in combination with temperature. The problem is the operators make so many adjustments that there is no steady state operation where I can determine the true effect of the variables."

"What do you mean too many adjustments, Tim? The operators have to make adjustments or we will never get the quality right," said Lou, who was the area manager.

"We learned there is such a thing as overcontrol, Lou. It's like driving a car. If you are constantly turning right and left you can't go in a straight line. But if you get the car going straight and only make small adjustments, you go straighter. Sort of take your hands off the steering wheel for a while."

"Oh come on, Tim. If the result is low you add some temperature, if it's high you take some off. How hard is that? I don't need Six Sigma to tell me that. Besides, I'm not sure I want to be here with you driving that kiln with your hands off the wheel," said Lou.

I said, "Don't worry, Lou, we will watch things closely. Tim already said he was not going to try and revolutionize the way we operate the kiln. As I understand it, he has several variables that he will run at high and low settings and we will let the kiln reach equilibrium. We run that way a while to get samples and we change to the next setting. That means no adjustments except to change to the next set points."

"Howard, are you going to let them do this? We are gonna make so much bad quality we will never be able to get rid of it all. We old production guys figured this kiln out 30 years ago and now these young kids think they are gonna computerize it and make it better," said Lou.

"I think it will be interesting," said Howard. "It's the only way to learn what is happening, Lou. If we put it off, it just takes that much longer to solve the problem. Do you know what it would mean for us to be able to dial in the surface area we want? It's a dream."

Lou just shook his head.

"Well, OK, if everyone says to do it I guess we gotta, but Jimmy, I am not promising anything on this week's schedule. No telling what we are going to make," said Lou.

Jimmy had not spoken until now. I wasn't sure what he was going to say or how he would react. As VP of sales, he would get the customer complaints.

"Go for it. It's an acceptable risk. If I have to delay customers at least I have a truthful reason to tell them this time. Usually, I just make reasons up."

We all laughed but it wasn't funny.

At the same time in a room on the other side of the plant, Ed was holding a meeting with his team. They had come to a crossroads on their filtration project and now they had to make a decision.

Ed said, "Folks, we have two possible ways to go. I don't know which one is the right way or if there is a right way. All I know is, Dave taught us that solving a problem is sometimes a process of elimination. We have to eliminate one of these possibilities. Our Pareto charts and PFMEA brought us to this point. We can work on changing the filter conditions or we can work on changing the composition of the feed to the filters. There are too many variables for us to do them both at the same time. It is a lot less risky to change the conditions of the filter so this is what I propose we do first. It has the least impact on the product and the plant."

The team took a vote and agreed with Ed. I had also followed Ed's problem closely. We knew the filtration area was a bottleneck. One thing that Ed discovered though was really unexpected. Especially since Ed was from maintenance and knew little about production.

When Ed's team developed their process map, they found a lot of built-in delays before filtration that were only there because everyone knew the filters were going to be down a lot anyway. For example, Ed found out that all of the reactors feeding the filtration area were shut down together for maintenance so that there was nothing moving forward. The only real reason they shut down the entire reactor area was so all the operators could go together to meetings or training sessions or take a break. It did not hurt anything because the filtration area could not keep up with the reactors with all the downtime. The reactor area just made up the inventory difference when they started back up.

The truth was, this maintenance downtime was built into the step capacities, so the reactor area on paper did not have any excess capacity. When the reactor operator on Ed's team heard they were fixing the filtration problem he told them his area was going to have to get on the ball too.

The operator explained how they could take advantage of the extra capacity immediately. There were numerous reactors and he said most of time when all the reactors were down, only two or three actually needed maintenance work. We had 12 reactors. This meant we had nine or 10 good reactors doing nothing for nearly 10 percent of the time when they could be making product. They were down only because of the filters.

If Ed's team could solve their problem with filtration, we could put the extra reactor capacity into the pipeline immediately. The only bottleneck downstream was selling the product, but since we would incur no additional fixed costs on the extra 10 percent, we could discount the price if need be and still make money.

It sounded a lot like Denise's project back at Nutech. The best part was we had an operator suggesting ideas that would make his job harder. That was a far cry from what we used to get. He told the team that if the executives could give up their cars, he could certainly give up some break time. Boy were times changing.

Tim's test on the kiln was into its second day now. Everyone was watching it since this was the first DOE we had done in the plant. So far, it was succeeding beyond my wildest dreams. I got a call that morning from Craig, who was helping monitor the test on midnights.

"Hey Barry, have you seen the production coming off #1 kiln for yesterday?" Craig asked.

"Not yet Craig, but it's 9 a.m., didn't you work midnights last night? Did your relief not show up?" I asked worried.

"No, no, Tony is here. I just wanted to stick around and see what happened when we switched to the next set of DOE conditions."

I could not believe my ears. Craig was always the first one out the gate when the whistle blew. He worked hard when he was here, but he was not going to spend one more minute out here than he had to. He was still here after working midnight shift. I found that beyond belief. I was speechless.

"You there, Barry? Hello? Hello?"

"I'm still here, Craig. How is the test going?"

"The kiln is running as steady as anyone has ever seen it. When we set up the first set of conditions, the quality started heading down. I mean I had to physically hold back the operator and the foreman from making an adjustment. I was worried myself, but Tim said to leave it alone."

"And then what happened?"

"It got to a point and then it started going back up all by itself. I mean we never touched anything. It climbed and then we thought it was going to get too high."

"Are you sure no one made any adjustments?"

"Positive, we have all the information from the computer system trended. Well it went down then up and finally it seemed to reach a sort of equilibrium. Just sort of flat-lined. I mean it changes from sample to sample but not like before."

"That's amazing, Craig. I'm going to come out and look at the trends myself. This I have to see."

When I got to the control room, there was no room to get in. It was packed with people. They were all staring at the computer terminal.

"OK, see here is where we started the test and this line is the product color and this one here is surface area." The operator who was on the Six Sigma team was explaining the graphs to the rest of the people.

"So what you are telling me, Bobby, is that no one made any adjustments for this eight hour period," Lou said skeptically.

"That's right, boss. Not a one. They wanted to, but Craig and me just wouldn't let them. I told them what Tim said and he was right." The operator was smiling from ear to ear.

Ted, the day production supervisor, was shaking his head. "Been here 20 years. Would not have believed it if I weren't seeing it with my own eyes. So what is happening now?"

Bobby hit a few buttons and a new page appeared on the computer screen. He also held up a clipboard. "These are the test conditions we are running. See we completed this one and now we are on the second set."

Ted looked at the clipboard. "Looks like we increased the temperature 10 degrees but we increased the rotation speed by a hair and increased the airflow all at the same time. Why in the world would we do that? That makes no sense to me at all!"

Tim had come in after taking some readings in the plant and started explaining, "This is part of the DOE, Ted. We have to see what happens as a result of these changes so we can determine how the variables of temperature, rotation speed, and airflow affect surface area and color."

"You mean you don't know what is going to happen and you're not trying to make it do something in particular?"

"You got it, Ted, right now we are simply learning about the patient. A little exploratory surgery. Once we run all of these conditions, I can plug in the data and the software will give us a model for how these variables affect our response variables, or Y variables as we call them. Those being surface area and color."

"But Tim," I said. "Isn't your project to improve surface area, not color?"

"Sure, Barry, but folks wouldn't be too happy if I improved surface area and messed up the color. That's what Dave called a lurking secondary variable. You have to be careful of those."

"I understand now. What has the second set of conditions done to us?"

"It's still early, but it seems that the surface area is getting higher and color has not changed. We need more time and samples though. We have to have enough data so that we take out some of the inherent variability in sampling and measurement."

"What do you mean?" I asked.

"Well, there is inherent error and variability in everything we do. So the more samples I get, the more accurate I can be."

"So if you take more samples instead of one, you can be more accurate."

"Basically, yes, Barry. The variability averages out so we have more confidence with larger sample sizes. You reach a point though where it just gets too expensive to take so many samples. We calculated four was right for this test."

Wow, I thought. All those tests we used to run where we made a change and took one sample and made a decision based on it. No wonder we used to think this process was art, not science.

"Good luck," I said as I headed back to my office. Craig was looking over Bobby's shoulder at the computer. He didn't even look tired after being up all night. I used to crash after my first midnight. I guess he was running on the excitement of the test.

28

Blackbelt Training: Control

The Blackbelts were back together for their last week of training. A few were worried about their projects being completed on time. Tom's project seemed to have hit a wall, but he was working hard on it. We had one of Dave's people coming in next week to work with him on it.

Richard also was struggling a little now. His team had selected what they thought was the best action plan, but now they had to reverse course and head out in a different direction. Dave said this was normal for some projects. Some are inherently more difficult than others. You didn't know until you had completed at least the first two months of training.

Tim's project was looking great and so was Ed's. Sarah was getting a handle on dispersion, but she had to come up with a whole new test before she could proceed so she was behind on her DOE phase.

Rodney was on track. Julie was bogging down a little, but she just needed more time. Carey and James were in good shape. The one I was most proud of was Paula. She was behind in the beginning due to no fault of her own. Her champion, Henry, from finance, had loaded her down with extra work. That had necessitated a stressful meeting but we had reached an understanding. She was now giving her presentation to the class.

"I think I'm back on track now, and the Six Sigma process is working. I have to admit to everyone that I felt like it was overkill for finance at first. But if I had not followed the road map we would never have gotten this far."

Paula was working on getting our money back from the customers faster, which was really critical for us because cash flow was a problem. The thing that usually kills a company is cash flow. It is amazing how much money is floating out there in space that can't be used.

We had gross sales of about 250 million dollars per year. We gave our customers net 30 days to pay us. Some paid on time, some paid late, and some never paid at all. We usually had about 40 million in receivables on the books or 60 days worth of sales. This was a huge amount of money to a company that was at best only breaking even most months. Paula's project was to get us our money faster.

"This is our Pareto chart of customer payment time in days," said Paula. "When we first started, I thought that with 300 customers there was no way I could do anything in four months. But the Pareto principle saved me. I would never have done this if I were not in a Six Sigma class. Finance people are not taught how to solve problems scientifically."

She continued, "This first chart shows how long the customers are taking to pay us. As you can see, out of 300 customers, 50 percent are paying in 30 days or less so we don't worry about them for now. That still left 150 customers, a huge number."

She continued, "Now this Pareto chart is for the remaining 150. It is based on the number of times they are late paying."

You can see that most have been late only a few times in the last couple years. That leaves about 20 percent that are late consistently. When I take that down another level and look at the actual dollars involved for these 20 percent, you see this."

Paula's third Pareto chart showed the remaining 60 customers that were frequently late paying. There were 10 customers that were big money and they paid terribly.

"You can see that these 10 customers are responsible for over 50 percent of the late receivables when you look at it from a dollar standpoint. Everyone in finance was amazed that it was so few customers and so much money."

"That is great, Paula, but why haven't we forced them to pay us on time? Don't we charge them interest or threaten them or something?" said James. "I know when I don't pay my bills on time I get threatening letters."

"Good point, James. Because these customers are so big, sales did not want us to do anything to make them mad. They were afraid we might lose the business. Finance would inform our salesperson and they were supposed to talk to the customer about paying on time."

I knew enough about sales to know that salespeople hate to rock the boat when the customer, especially a big one, is buying. Our salespeople got a nice commission in addition to their salary and these customers represented a pretty fat bonus check for someone. I was sure they said they were discussing it but I had my doubts that there was much pressure involved.

"So what are we going to do, Paula? We can't make our biggest customers mad," said Sarah.

"We agree, and our team came up with what we think is an innovative approach. We are doing a test, not really a DOE, but still a test. We are offering a small discount to these big customers if they pay on time or early. We will see what it does for us. The discount will cost us a little, but if we can get them paying us on time, it can improve our cash flow significantly."

"How much will it cost, Paula?"

"Without going into a big financial discussion, it represents about 20 percent of what it costs us to borrow the money, which is what we do until we get our money. Based on current interest rates, it will cost us about $50,000 per year but we will save $250,000 per year in interest charges. Plus our cash flow will improve significantly."

"Wow. $200,000 savings per year for that. We work our tails off in production to save that," said Rodney.

"That is very conservative too. We have ideas for the smaller customers that can double that amount. It just requires more time than I have right now."

"Sounds great, Paula. Good work. What does Henry think about this?" I replied.

"Funny you should ask. He wanted me to ask you if he can put two people from finance in the next Blackbelt class," she said, laughing.

— ◢ ◣ —

Dave had sent in someone special named Martin to teach the last module. He was an expert in advanced DOE topics. Although the module was named control, he explained there was a lot of tweaking you could do that was critical to better control.

The Blackbelts had no problem understanding it. I did not have a clue myself. They discussed things like *steepest ascent*, *response surface methodology*, and *custom designed factorials*. Martin told me that all of the modules built on one another so it was like trying to learn calculus without knowing algebra first. He reminded me that was what the Blackbelts were for. My job was to lead them and point them at the projects that had the most impact, not to perform the experiments.

I was able to pick up a lot even if I didn't understand it all. Seldom did one DOE ever tell you everything you needed to know. It was like opening a large box that had other boxes inside. Every test got you one step deeper in finding the jewel at the bottom of the smallest box. The number of boxes you had to open had to do with a lot of things, but when you reached the limits of your measurement error you had to stop.

To improve further, you had to improve your test first. Martin said he had the hardest time teaching this simple concept to people. It was no different than using a microscope. With better and better magnification you can see more and more things. In other words, you cannot see what you cannot test accurately for.

He asked me if we had a program in place to improve our test methods. I told him no. He was not surprised since even the best companies ignored their measurement systems. Measurement is the key to improvement, he said. With a better microscope no telling what we might discover.

29

The Results Roll In

The Blackbelts had finished their four weeks of training and were deep into completing their projects. Most would require more than three weeks to finish up, which was normal according to Dave. This is why they told people it was a five-month commitment instead of four. In the end it took a lot of time to get everything completed and issue a report.

Tim, my superstar from R&D, was making a presentation to management about his project on the surface area control on #1 kiln. Jack was there along with Steve, Howard, Henry, Jimmy, Mark, and myself.

Tim said, "I was very excited to hear about the advanced DOE tools in the last class and I can tell you that what I have done so far is the tip of the iceberg when it comes to controlling those kilns."

I thought back to when I had forced Mark to give me Tim as a Blackbelt instead of Donald. I was so glad I had done that, and now Mark was too, but I doubt he would admit it. Tim had so much confidence in himself and his abilities now.

"Barry will be happy to hear we now have in place a *real* SPC chart," Tim said clapping. "One we actually control with and the operators understand, and use. In fact, now they are begging for charts on the other kilns. Seems they don't trust their own instincts anymore."

"Hooray for Tim," I said, clapping too.

We all now knew what a real SPC chart could do for us. Our capability had improved by 40 percent when we quit making so many adjustments and used the chart for what it was intended. I mean, it was ridiculous what we trying to do before. Control a process with an SPC chart when we didn't even know what to adjust when it went out of control. We just played connect the dots before.

I for one was actually looking forward to our next ISO 9001 audit. Man would that auditor be surprised. I sure hoped they couldn't take away our ISO registration for what we used to do. We were in great shape now with ISO.

Mark was so proud of Tim he could hardly quit smiling. He had turned into a Six Sigma fanatic who seemed to be able to talk about nothing else. Maybe his higher level of education kept him from believing until he saw it happen in real life. He was like a smoker who had quit smoking and could not stop telling everyone else they ought to stop. But now he was almost as irritating on the other side of the fence as he was when he hated Six Sigma. Go figure.

My QC lab manager, Sarah, had her project in overdrive right now. The test at CMG, our favorite customer, turned out to be a good one and this meant she could move into the improve phase. Of course she had to train all of the technicians on the new test and inform all of the customers of the change. There were specification issues and ISO issues; it was a mess, but she was getting it done. People didn't understand that these side issues were what took so much time, but they had to be done. She was scheduled to do her DOE in the plant next week.

I was really proud of our Blackbelt from maintenance. Ed's project was nearly complete. He had made the right choice in working on filtration conditions. His DOE involved studying the effects of vacuum, drum speed, drum level, and filter cloth porosity. He came up with an innovative way to test different porosity cloths by having a special one made up by the vendor. I remembered the one I had seen in Bill's office in 1985. Bill had sent the thing back and they could not find anything wrong with it. The cloth was one of the items that still showed up high on Ed's Pareto chart for downtime.

Ed still had to run a couple more tests but he was sure he had a solution that would allow us to take advantage of the extra reactor capacity.

As a production supervisor, Rodney's project was important not only because of the money it could save us, but because it proved to everyone that you did not need to be a college graduate to solve problems using Six Sigma. There would be savings, about $35,000 per year, but it also solved a headache that had bugged production for years. When the dryer flamed out, it meant product had to be dumped on the ground and shoveled up by operators. It was a terrible job they all hated.

Rodney had solved the problems by instituting new maintenance and operating procedures. It sent a message that Six Sigma was something everyone in the plant could be a part of. We had lots of hourly people wanting to be Greenbelts because of Rodney.

Julie, our newest employee from R&D, saw her project getting more interesting each day. When she started looking at the improvements James was making in residue control and Tim was making in surface area control, the idea Russ had of producing to-order started to make sense.

Her Pareto chart showed we did not have nearly as many special requests as we thought. She had worked with some of the customers and gotten them to standardize on certain packaging materials. It seemed all we had to do was explain the problem and ask, and a lot of them were willing to work with us.

The logistics company she had involved showed her how to use bar coding to track the inventory better. Now she was putting her ideas in place and working with sales and production on planning next month's shipments. She thought we could reduce our inventory stocking levels by half and not have any problems meeting orders. That was going to save big money. And she only had three month's experience at our plant when she started the project.

Richard from Purchasing was still struggling some with his project. After the early results, it turned out to be harder than we all thought. He had managed to reduce the loss of the raw material blowing away by using the spray again. This was going to net us about $15,000 a year. He was working on a big loss with another raw material, but it required a change by the supplier and they were behind in what they promised him. He was still going to meet his goals but he knew there was a lot more to be had.

Carey's project had more to do about staying in business than it did about saving money. He worked for environmental, and we had received several warnings from the EPA about effluent violations for pH. Carey had systematically used the tools to come up with a plan to reduce emissions and was putting it in place. If nothing else, Six Sigma sure made you prepared and organized.

When Carey and the environmental manager presented the project to the local EPA, they started wanting to know about Six Sigma. It seemed the government needed some help getting things done too. Not that this would be startling information to most taxpayers.

— —

The project James, who worked in engineering, had initiated to reduce the residue level had turned into that and more. He became so fascinated with the project that Bill had tried in 1985, he tried it again. It worked this time so we were finally going to get the half million in savings a year. But now it worked out to nearly three-quarters of a million due to inflation. Our plant engineering department was so convinced of successful returns on investments now, they asked corporate to increase our capital allotment for next year and guaranteed a return of one year on the money. It seemed that Six Sigma had given them some confidence when it came to sticking out their necks a little.

— —

Paula's finance project was essentially finished but she refused to stop. She had met all of her goals since it seemed even big corporations had a hard time turning down a discount. They were paying before the 30 days were over to be sure the check did not get held up and cost them the discount.

She was putting her second phase in operation now with the smaller customers. Henry was so impressed with her work that he was considering her for the cost accounting manager job when Jackie retired in a few months.

Henry had told me in confidence that he never thought much of Paula and that was why he gave her to the Blackbelt program. It turned out she was just shy, and intimidated by Henry's management style. Given the chance, she excelled and had a lot more confidence in herself too.

Tom was the last Blackbelt. He worked for Jimmy in technical service. His project was different than the others in that the savings were more difficult to put a value on. We had always had a hard time developing new products for the paper industry. We needed a way to screen our ideas better because it was such a long product development cycle and so expensive to run trials on a paper machine.

Also, there were so many variables and problems in papermaking that we were never sure if our new products worked or not. The paper machines were so big, they went through our trial amounts like a kid eating candy.

Tom had developed several tests that would provide nearly instant feedback. This way we could use the Design for Six Sigma methods and turn out some hot new products. How do you put a value on that?

Dave had suggested a big finish to our first training class by having a project fair for the plant to attend and then a certification ceremony and dinner at a nice place. It really made the right statement to the Blackbelts and everyone else at the plant.

I was tracking all of the projects and writing an article for each issue of our plant newsletter. It kept the interest level high. I found out that you simply cannot communicate enough.

30

Certification

It was now almost five months after we had started training our first wave of Blackbelts. And it was approaching a year since I had met Russ and first learned about Six Sigma. This past year had flown by quickly, but we had accomplished more than in any other year I could remember. Sure we had had successes before, but I think those had more to do with luck than science. For the first time in my career, we really understood what was happening in several parts of our plant. Even more important, I think everyone now believed that we had a lot to learn about our plant.

Maybe this was the secret of Six Sigma. It changed the mind-set of people. We had gone from thinking our plant was somehow different to knowing we were not different. We thought scientific principles did not apply to us, and now we knew our problem had been our lack of knowledge. We used to think our people didn't care about making things better. Now we knew that management had been holding them back. We used to think it took five years experience before someone could contribute, and now we only needed five months. Managers used to fight over everything and now it seemed we seldom disagreed. We used to look for someone to blame and now we looked for the solution. For me though, the best part was looking forward to going to work instead of dreading it.

We had reserved the big dining room at the Hilton for the certification dinner. We debated over whom to invite and like most recognition functions, you did not want to leave anyone out, but there was a limit too. Things have a way of getting out of hand if you are not careful.

We were absolutely certain we wanted the Blackbelts and all their team members. Ultimately, we decided to include all the champions even though that doubled the head count. This was not a time to put any doubt in people's minds over our support.

Earlier in the day, we had our project fair. This was done on the plant site so everyone that wanted to attend had a chance to come. The ten Blackbelts had set up display tables about their projects. The tables had visual aids, a copy of their final report, and selected graphs and pictures from their projects. Russ had encouraged us to take pictures of our team members during the projects and the response of the people was amazing. I still don't know what it was about seeing your picture displayed that had such an effect on people, but Russ was certainly right.

I don't know how many of the plant employees attended, but there was a steady stream of people coming and going. You could hear people congratulating each other for a good job, but I was most interested in those people attending the fair that had not originally shown an interest in Six Sigma. Dave told me that if I could get enough people supporting Six Sigma—a critical mass—the rest would follow. As far as I could tell, the "rest" were showing up in droves.

"Hey Bobby, you were on Julie's team weren't you?" said Amy. Amy and Bobby worked together in the warehouse.

"Yeah, come on over and I'll introduce you to Julie and show you what we did for this company." Bobby pulled Amy towards Julie's table.

"Julie, this is Amy. We work together in the warehouse."

"Hi, Amy, very nice to meet you. Has Bobby told you how much help he was to us on our project?"

Amy replied, "That's all he has talked about for the last five months. Julie said this and Six Sigma that. We got tired of hearing it. But that's just Bobby for ya. Running his mouth all the time." Bobby was smiling ear to ear.

Julie continued, "Well, there's a second Blackbelt training class starting up soon and we will have a lot more projects underway. Of course all of us in the first class are working on more projects too. We would love to have you on one of our project teams."

"Well, I'll think about it," said Amy as she walked off with Bobby to look at another project.

"By the way, Bobby," Amy remarked, "Why are you all dressed up tonight? You aren't a Blackbelt. All you did was go to a few team meetings."

"I may not be the Blackbelt, but I am an important part of the team. That's why I will be dining at the Hilton tonight and you will be chowing down at McDonalds."

"What, you must be kidding! They invited the team members too. This company has never recognized any of us working stiffs. If I had known that, I would have volunteered for one of the teams. Probably feed y'all pretty good too, I bet."

"Prime rib and shrimp is what I heard."

"You tell your Six Sigma friends, they'd better ask me to be on a team for the next class."

"Tell them yourselves. They asked for volunteers, so I joined. But you better volunteer quickly this next time. I have a feeling the spots are going to go fast. Plus I already told them I wanted to be on every team in our area anyway."

"You are such a hog, Bobby." Amy leaned over and whispered to Bobby. "Who do I need to talk to to get on a team?"

From across the room, I saw Bobby pointing his finger toward me.

—— ——

During dinner, the sounds of people and talking and laughing reverberated throughout the room. I glanced at my watch; the time had come to start the presentations. I looked at Dave and Bob and pointed to the podium. We all started to the front of the room.

"You guys ready to get started?" I said.

"Absolutely," said Bob. Dave nodded yes.

As I stepped up to the podium, it was not even necessary to ask people to stop talking. The room got incredibly quiet and all eyes were on me. My hands were shaking a little as I leaned forward slightly to speak into the microphone.

"Let me be the first to thank everyone for coming tonight. This may feel like the end of something, but it is really only the beginning."

My introduction lasted only a few minutes, but when I was through I was not nervous any longer. Bob, Dave, and I presented each Blackbelt with a nice plaque that certified them as a Six Sigma Blackbelt. In addition, Jack presented each one with a $500 bonus check.

Then each of the Blackbelts recognized their team members and presented them with a nice jacket and a $100 bonus check. We had argued over whether we should give team members money or certificates or nothing. A few people felt we were setting some kind of bad precedent by giving out money; people would walk around with their hands out when they were already getting a paycheck. Russ said we were overreacting and we were going to save millions, why be so concerned about a few thousand dollars. He was right of course, as usual.

—— ——

I had asked several people to give short speeches but the most memorable were near the end. Henry was visibly nervous as he faced the crowd.

"First of all, I want to say that I was not a proponent of Six Sigma in the beginning. I agreed to it because we had a new president that seemed to like it and I didn't want to get on his bad side." He looked over and smiled at Bob.

"I really could not see how the finance department could play a role in something like Six Sigma. But because of Paula and all of the other Blackbelts, I can now see how important the finance department is, in not only this, but in the overall success of this company. Before Six Sigma, I saw our role in finance as that of an outside auditor keeping score of what everyone else did, but not really responsible for making things happen. Now I see our function as focusing the organization in the right direction and driving the changes and improvements."

Mark was the next person to speak.

"Well, if Henry says he was not a proponent of Six Sigma, I guess that means I was an opponent. I had been through so many programs that I had become a cynic, stuck in the past. It took a young engineer like Tim to prove to me that making pigment was indeed a science and not an art. He has renewed my enthusiasm for research and development. I am excited to be a part of this new organization."

I had asked Bob to give the closing comments but he refused saying that I should have that honor. So I said what was on my mind.

"Ladies and gentlemen, we are really at a crossroads in the history of our plant. Never in my wildest imagination did I think we could achieve so much in such a short period of time. These 10 Blackbelts have saved us a lot of money, but they have done so much more than that. The biggest thing I see is they have provided a means to take our people and give them the tools to make immediate impact on our business and profitability. When I first started here nearly 20 years ago, I was told it would take five years before I could even start contributing. Now we take someone with five months experience and challenge him or her to solve our toughest problems. And best of all, they can do it!"

I continued, "It has also brought management and the workforce together with a common goal. Instead of adversaries, we are now teammates. I am not naïve enough to believe that we are anywhere close to where we need to be in terms of efficiency and cost or quality. But we do have a method that we can use to get us there. This is our challenge."

I found it was easy to speak when you believed in what you were saying.

"I think the last five months has taught us we must never get too old to learn or listen to new ways of doing things. We must encourage our people to learn new skills and to look for better ways of doing things."

I paused to let my statements sink in. I certainly had the attention of our audience.

"There is one negative thing I can say about Six Sigma." I saw several people sit up in their chairs and a few raised brows.

I continued, smiling, "I am becoming increasingly less tolerant of poor quality and poor service from our suppliers and the world in general. If we can make things better in our plant, so could everyone else. Until now, I never realized how poor the service was at most places, how unprepared people are to help you, and how little people seem to care."

I saw people nodding their heads and talking to their friends.

"I think we can say that our expectations have increased. We intend to discuss with our suppliers how they can help us improve. We rely so much on them that we cannot reach our goals without their help. Just think of the possibilities we have with them helping us and us helping them, instead of just fighting over price."

"In conclusion, I want to thank each of you personally for your help in making this first part of our journey from art to science a great success."

31

Three Months Later

Jimmy sat across from my desk as we discussed the new opportunity that had presented itself to us. When he had called earlier and asked to meet with me, I could tell that he was excited about something. Now I was getting as excited as he was.

"OK, what you are telling me then, Jimmy, is that we can substantially increase our volume to CMG Coatings if they get this aerospace contract that is up for bid."

"Exactly, Barry. Sarah's first Blackbelt project identified a problem with their milling step as well as a problem with our dispersion testing. Now that they know how to operate their equipment better, they can meet the tighter specifications for the bid. Before, they never even considered bidding on such a contract."

"And you think they have a chance at getting this big a contract?" I asked skeptically.

"Absolutely, Barry. Since you got CMG off and running on their own Six Sigma implementation, they have been learning a lot about themselves. And don't forget—the customer, Strata Systems, has been doing Six Sigma for years."

"Well what do we have to do to help CMG get the business?" I couldn't see how we could help a customer get business.

Jimmy smiled. "The main thing CMG has to do is be competitive on the bid. Don't you have folks from our major raw material suppliers in the second Blackbelt class?"

"Sure, Jimmy, but how does that help?" We had included several of our key suppliers in the second wave of Blackbelts.

"Don't you see, Barry? Our costs are based on not only what we do but also what our suppliers do. If we can involve our raw material suppliers, we can be more competitive with the pigments and the catalysts for the coatings. CMG has the equipment and expertise to make the coating and then they can be more competitive on the coatings bid. If we work with our suppliers and our customer, we are sure to get the business."

It hit me like a ton of bricks. "Oh, I see what you mean. We are all Six Sigma companies needing the same thing. Strata Systems needs a low-cost, high-quality coating. CMG needs the business making the coating. HPZ needs the pigment and catalyst volume. And our suppliers need to sell us the raw materials. We can all win if we work together."

"Now you got it. What do you think? If we can form a Six Sigma team with representatives from all four groups, think what we might come up with."

"What we can come up with, Jimmy, is a way to increase our sales by 10 percent and capture a piece of the market we never have been able to play in. Long-term, the profit margins in this area should be better for us too."

"Absolutely, Barry. It can really jump-start our business this year. I'm happy we are making a little money again, but this is a way we can start making some real profit. I'm not satisfied any more with just staying in business. I want to grow."

"I know what you mean, Jimmy. I've been itching to hit a home run too. I will talk to our suppliers tomorrow and Dennis from CMG to see what they think."

"OK, well I'll get with the salespeople from CMG and see if they want to schedule a meeting with Strata Systems. I think we should make a joint presentation to Strata with representatives from all of our companies. Sound OK?"

"Sounds great, Jimmy."

"Last thing, Barry. You are absolutely certain we can make the new pigment and catalyst needed for this aerospace coating consistently in specification for CMG if we get the business."

I smiled at Jimmy. "A year ago I would have been screaming at you for even suggesting something like this, but not now. Here are the capability studies for the product coming from #1 kiln and the control charts for the reactors on the catalyst production line."

Jimmy leaned over and looked at the statistical charts. We all looked at data differently now. Since we had standardized on the Six Sigma methods, we all knew what we were seeing and how to interpret it.

"Boy, the capability for surface area is fantastic now. We can control easily to plus or minus one point," Jimmy replied.

"Better than that, Jimmy. Tim also figured out how to control the process so we can also shift the mean to anywhere between 11 and 32 and still maintain that capability."

"Wow," said Jimmy. "Now I see what you mean. We can produce in regions we never thought were possible for our equipment."

"Exactly, and the catalyst reactors are in control so that product is consistent too."

Jimmy looked at the SPC charts for the reactors. "Nothing but random variation. But look how tight the control limits are now."

"That's because before we had so much variability in the testing that we had no clue what was happening. The real reason we can even think about this, though, is Ed's project at filtration."

Jimmy nodded his head. "That's right, if he had not corrected the filter problems, we wouldn't even be able to use the extra reactor capacity to go after the new business."

"Jimmy, notice how all of these projects added up to us being able to do something we never even considered when we started the individual projects?"

"Yeah, I was thinking the same thing."

"It really just shows that the pursuit of improvement and knowledge about our business is always necessary. Even if we don't know exactly at the time we do it what the real return on our investment will be."

"I know what you mean, Barry. We used to say we needed a reason to get better—a big payoff—before we decided to spend our time improving. How stupid we used to be. I mean, you can't predict future opportunities."

"I agree, Jimmy, you can't predict the future but you can predict one thing."

"What's that, Barry?"

"The more you know about what makes your process tick, the better you can see the opportunities for reducing costs and making better product. Then when opportunities like this happen, you can take advantage of them. We used to always be one step behind. When new business like this used to present itself, what would happen?"

Jimmy thought for a second. "We would have so much to do to be able to get the business we would be too late or even worse . . . we would say we could do it, struggle to make it happen, do a poor job, and then lose the business anyway. And the customer would get so mad they would never buy from us again."

"You got it. You really can't afford *not* to continuously improve all the time because you never know what opportunity is just over the horizon. And it's so simple anyway. When you are the low-cost and high-quality producer, you seldom lose."

Jimmy said, "You know, we were lucky, Barry."

"What do you mean, lucky? We worked hard to get to this point."

"Sure, hard work was a lot of it. But think about all of the things that had to happen for this to be successful."

"I know what you mean. If we had never had the problem with Nutech I would never have met Russ. Without him, I doubt we would have even given Six Sigma a shot—we wouldn't have understood it. I mean, I am just now understanding what it is all about."

"Yep, and how about the fact that Bob showed up when he did as president. We both know that if he had not been here to support us, Jack would have never gone for Six Sigma. Plus, Jack just doesn't command that type of respect from the people. You hear people saying stuff has to be supported from the top to succeed. It is true, but most managers have no idea what that really means."

"And we would have *never* gotten Jack to agree to sell the company cars," I laughed.

Jimmy exclaimed, "You are right there! I think that was a key part in our success now, too. I had to give up my car and at first I couldn't see how that would make a difference in people's attitudes. I thought, what's the big deal? The amount of money tied up in those cars is just a drop in the bucket compared to what we spend every day."

"Perception, Jimmy. It is the perception of the people that is so important. Small money or not, those cars were perceived by the people to be important. So they were." This I was absolutely convinced about.

"And what about Dave and his people from Six Sigma Enterprises? They were excellent. I'm sure there are Six Sigma trainers out there that are not so good. We were lucky to get them."

"Yeah, we were lucky because we didn't know what we were doing, and we had let ourselves get so far behind. But think about if we had had the foresight to have done something like Six Sigma 10 years or even five years ago. Where would we be now?"

"I don't even want to think about it, Barry. It's just too depressing. But you are right. If we had started earlier when our business was not so bad, we might be the industry leader now. And luck would have had nothing to do with it."

I reflected on my professional career. For nearly 20 years I had been a participant in this rat race we call the business world. But now I felt like the first 20 years had all been preparation for the next 20 years. I believed in myself and had no doubt that I was prepared to make a difference. The reason was not Six Sigma. It was what Six Sigma was allowing me to do. The difference was me and all of the other people that shared our common goal of continuous improvement.

I had a feeling that the next 20 years were going to be a lot more fun than the previous 20 years.